Tampa Bay Rays IQ: The Ultimate Test of True Fandom

Andy Sonnanstine & Tucker Elliot

2011 Edition (Volume I)

Printed in the United States of America.
Copyright © 2011 by Andy Sonnanstine & Tucker Elliot.

This title is part of the IQ sports trivia book series, which is a trademark of Black Mesa Publishing, LLC.

Cataloging-in-Publication Data is available from the Library of Congress.

ISBN: 978-0-9826759-7-7
First edition, first printing.

Cover design by Holly Ross.

Black Mesa Publishing, LLC
Florida
David Horne and Marc CB Maxwell
Black.Mesa.Publishing@gmail.com

www.blackmesabooks.com

Contents

Introduction 1

First 3

Second 15

Third 25

Fourth 37

Fifth 49

Sixth 63

Seventh 73

Eighth 85

Ninth 95

Free Baseball! 107

About the Authors 119

Acknowledgements 121

References 123

About Black Mesa 125

I would like to dedicate this book to all the important people who have helped me achieve my dream.
— A.S.

"We're the city Sports Illustrated *called a loser. We're the city that's been called an Albanian village ... St. Petersburg has arrived. We are Major League today.*"

— David Fischer, St. Petersburg mayor, after his city was awarded the Rays' franchise on March 9, 1995

"The one thing about it, and what I try to tell people, they think the Rays are finally competitive. Even through the early years, when the team was losing 90 to 100 games, it was still a competitive team. If your definition of competitive is all about whether your team is winning ball games, that's one thing. But if your definition is every night when I step on the field you think you have a chance to win, that's something else. You may lose that game, but ... the Rays have always been a competitive team. Just this year they've won more games."

— Fred McGriff, after the Tampa Bay Rays clinched the 2008 American League Pennant

Courtesy author.

Introduction

IT HAS ALWAYS been a dream of mine to see my name on the back of a Major League Baseball jersey, and for the past seven years, that dream has been a reality with the Tampa Bay Rays. The Rays are an amazing organization, and it has been an honor and a privilege to be a part of this team.

However, I never imagined viewing my name on the cover of a book, as the author.

When I was presented with the opportunity to collaborate on the eighth baseball book in the IQ Sport Series, I was extremely excited. Now, through The Ultimate Test of True Fandom, I am able to reach out to our fans and test their knowledge on the Rays, a team we all love and support. To be given this opportunity is truly a dream come true, allowing me to combine my passions for baseball, writing and photography.

We have divided the book into nine chapters, just like the innings in a real game—and as a bonus, we've thrown in a tenth chapter for extra-innings. In the top of each frame we begin with an intro highlighting extraordinary moments and players in Rays' history—and then in both the top and bottom of each inning you will have the opportunity to test your own trivia skills. No pressure, but we will keep score after each inning!

Is your brain as strong as your brawn?

It won't take long to find out, but in the first inning we start things off easy and give you some "minor league" questions that even a fair-weathered fan should be able to answer. Make sure you take advantage of these questions to pad your score, because as the game progresses it's just like being called up to "The Show" where everything is tougher competing under the glow of the lights.

By the time the seventh-inning stretch comes along and fans are all singing *Take Me Out to the Ball Game*, are you still going to be in the line-up? Only one way to find out ... bring your A-game and leave it all on the field!

I can guarantee that this book will bring back great memories, as we re-live some of the greatest moments in Rays' history. It will also put into perspective how unbelievable our rise to the top of the toughest division in baseball has been.

Over the next nine innings you will be challenged to answer questions that chronicle our relatively short, but much storied 13-year history of Rays Baseball. Now it's your turn to try for what few players in baseball have ever accomplished—The Perfect Game!

Andy Sonnanstine
St. Petersburg, FL
March 2011

First

MAJOR LEAGUE BASEBALL has been in Florida for nearly a century in the form of Spring Training—and professional baseball has been in the Tampa-St. Pete area since 1908 when the Cincinnati Reds played an exhibition game against the semi-pro St. Petersburg Saints. Just five years later the Chicago Cubs began conducting Spring Training at Plant Field in Tampa, and by the 1920s training sites for Major League teams were being built all across the state from Jacksonville to Tampa to Fort Myers to West Palm Beach. The premiere training facility, however, was Sunshine Park in St. Petersburg. It held 5,000 fans and was built with state of the art batting cages and all the amenities necessary for a Major League team to prepare for the upcoming season.

And when the Phillies used Sunshine Park in 1915 and then proceeded to win 14 of 15 games to start the regular season, well ... let's just say that's the moment that Florida cemented it's reputation as Major League Baseball's spring training capital.

The Tampa-St. Pete area witnessed more than its fair share of baseball legends throughout the decades, but it wasn't until MLB teams voted unanimously on March 9, 1995, to accept the Tampa Bay Devil Rays and the Arizona Diamondbacks as the 13th and 14th expansion teams in Major League history that this Mecca of the baseball world had a team all its own. The Devil Rays began play in 1998, and the club became the first in baseball's modern era (since 1901) to host spring training in its home city—St. Petersburg.

Tampa, like any other expansion team, toiled and persevered in its infancy—but today, minus the Devil, the Rays have become one of the most exciting teams in baseball. The "Ten Innings" in this book will take you through every season of Rays' history—but here in the First, we begin with some questions about

Tampa's most recent stars whose exploits on the field of play have made the Rays a force to be reckoned with in the American League's Eastern Division.

>   Longoria, Upton, Crawford, Zobrist, Peña ...
>   Price, Shields, Garza, Davis, Kazmir ...
>   Here we go. Time to keep score.
>   *Play ball!*

TOP OF THE FIRST

QUESTION 1: This Rays' player is accustomed to receiving high accolades from the press, fans, teammates, and peers from around baseball—however, in 2010, he elevated his game even more and garnished some serious hardware in the offseason as a result. Who earned his first career Gold Glove Award and his first career Silver Slugger Award in 2010?

    a)   Evan Longoria
    b)   Carlos Peña
    c)   Carl Crawford
    d)   Ben Zobrist

QUESTION 2: Tampa began play on August 16, 2010, tied for first in the A.L. East with the New York Yankees and facing a stiff challenge to stay on top with the Texas Rangers in town and Cliff Lee on the mound. This player, however, made sure the Rays didn't give up any ground to the Yanks. Texas carried a 4-2 lead into the bottom of the eighth with Lee still going strong, but he delivered a clutch RBI single that tied the game 4-4 and ignited a four-run rally to lift the Rays to a 6-4 victory. And he was just getting started, too. He batted .393 with three multi-hit games and three multi-RBI games as the Rays swept Texas and posted a 5-2 record for the week. Texas manager Ron Washington said, "He had a great series. We couldn't stop him from the first game on." For his great stats he earned Bank of America's Player of the Week honors. Who is this clutch hitter?

a) Evan Longoria
b) Carlos Peña
c) Carl Crawford
d) Ben Zobrist

QUESTION 3: This pitcher won Bank of America's Player of the Week honors after he tossed the first no-hitter in franchise history on July 26, 2010, vs. the Detroit Tigers. Tampa had been no-hit three times since 2009, two of them perfect games, prompting him to say, "We needed one. I don't care who it came from. We just needed one for our own confidence. The guys are just as excited as I am. It's fun ... the defense made great plays. I really can't say enough about them." At least as important as the no-hitter was the fact he kept the Rays in the playoff hunt by winning his fourth consecutive decision. Who is this pitcher?

a) David Price
b) Wade Davis
c) James Shields
d) Matt Garza

QUESTION 4: The week beginning June 14, 2010, was especially good to this Rays' player. He won his third career Bank of America Player of the Week honors, posting some pretty gaudy numbers: .810 slugging percentage, .571 on-base percentage, nine runs, three multi-hit games, four extra-base hits, and three steals— all on the road during interleague play. Not to mention he contributed on defense with some spectacular plays, as well. He also made his fourth All-Star team in 2010. Who is this player?

a) Carlos Peña
b) Carl Crawford
c) B.J. Upton
d) Pat Burrell

QUESTION 5: This pitcher won American League Pitcher of the Month honors in September 2010 after posting a

4-0 record with a 1.67 earned run average, and striking out 33 batters in six starts. Opponents hit just .175 against him in 43 innings of work. And as a bonus he also tossed eight scoreless innings with eight strikeouts vs. Baltimore on September 28 to clinch a playoff spot for the Rays. Who is this star pitcher?

- a)   David Price
- b)   Wade Davis
- c)   James Shields
- d)   Matt Garza

QUESTION 6: He won Player of the Month honors in June 2010 after batting .324 with a league best ten doubles. In 26 games he also hit five homers, scored 20 runs, drove home 22, posted a .394 on-base percentage and a .562 slugging percentage, and he also stole a league best 14 bases. When asked about the award he replied, "I've been swinging the bat well lately ... it feels good, but you can't dwell on it too long. Embrace it while you have the chance, then move on, keep trying to get better." Who is this star player?

- a)   Carlos Peña
- b)   Carl Crawford
- c)   B.J. Upton
- d)   Ben Zobrist

QUESTION 7: He began 2009 on a torrid clip, batting .369 with six homers and 24 RBIs in April, and as a result he earned Player of the Month honors. This star slugger also led the Major Leagues with 11 doubles, 17 extra-base hits, and 60 total bases. "I'd take a win over anything and I'd much rather us be in first place," he said of the award. "The personal accomplishments are something that I'll be able to treasure by myself for the rest of my life." Who is this slugger?

- a)   Carlos Peña
- b)   Carl Crawford

c) Pat Burrell
d) Evan Longoria

QUESTION 8: This pitcher became the first player in Rays' history to earn a monthly award when he won Pitcher of the Month honors in May 2008. After suffering an injury in February that caused him to miss the first month of the season, he made his season debut on May 4 but suffered a loss to the Red Sox at Fenway Park. He didn't let that discourage him though, instead he reeled off five straight victories with a microscopic 0.55 earned run average the rest of the month. Overall he was 5-1 with a 1.22 ERA and 38 strikeouts in 37 innings of work. He was also the first pitcher in team history to record five wins in a single month. He closed out the month by striking out ten and holding the Rangers to three hits in seven innings on May 26, prompting Texas manager Ron Washington to say, "He shut our whole lineup down ... he could shut anybody down the way he pitched." Who is this award-winning pitcher?
a) Scott Kazmir
b) Andy Sonnanstine
c) James Shields
d) Edwin Jackson

QUESTION 9: He won Bank of America's Player of the Week honors three times in 2009. The third time he won the award was for the week beginning August 31, when he led the league with a .467 average and three homers—and eight of his 14 hits went for extra-bases. Who is this slugger?
a) B.J. Upton
b) Gabe Gross
c) Evan Longoria
d) Carlos Peña

QUESTION 10: During the week beginning June 15, 2009, Twins' outfielder Michael Cuddyer had four multi-hit games, Rangers' second baseman Ian Kinsler hit a league best three homers, and Tigers' first baseman Miguel Cabrera led the league with nine RBIs. All great numbers to be sure—but none of them as great as the numbers put up by this Rays' player, who won American League Player of the Week honors for the second time in his career. In six games he was 12 for 28 at the plate (.429 average), with three doubles, two homers, and two steals. Twice that week he was a triple short of the cycle. Who is this slugger?

    a)   B.J. Upton
    b)   Gabe Gross
    c)   Evan Longoria
    d)   Carlos Peña

TOP OF THE FIRST ANSWER KEY

___ QUESTION 1: C
___ QUESTION 2: A
___ QUESTION 3: D
___ QUESTION 4: B
___ QUESTION 5: A
___ QUESTION 6: C
___ QUESTION 7: D*
___ QUESTION 8: A
___ QUESTION 9: C
___ QUESTION 10: A

KEEP A RUNNING TALLY OF YOUR CORRECT ANSWERS!

Number correct: ___ / 10

Overall correct: ___ / 10

#7 – Carlos Peña also received consideration for this award after he belted nine homers with 24 RBIs on the month.

BOTTOM OF THE FIRST

QUESTION 11: Tampa's offense might have struggled with a low average (13th in the league) and high strikeouts (first in the league) in 2010, but it wasn't because of a lack of effort from this player. He led the league in triples and was among the top ten league leaders in hits, average, runs, and steals—and due in large part to his success, the Rays' offense was third in the league in runs, second in triples, and first in steals. Who was this catalyst to the Rays' 2010 offense?

    a)   B.J. Upton
    b)   Ben Zobrist
    c)   Evan Longoria
    d)   Carl Crawford

QUESTION 12: This player earned Gillette's Rookie of the Month honors for the Rays after batting .300 with eight homers, 19 RBIs, and a healthy .650 slugging percentage during his third month in the big leagues. Manager Joe Maddon said, "He's still understanding the Major League game and what they are trying to do to him. As he gains more confidence in that regard, I know he's going to get better." Who is this player?

    a)   B.J. Upton
    b)   Ben Zobrist
    c)   Evan Longoria
    d)   Carl Crawford

QUESTION 13: After a 4-1 loss to Minnesota at home on September 21, 2008, Tampa saw its lead in the A.L. East slip to just 1.5 games over the Boston Red Sox. Worse, the Rays then had to hit the road for the season's final week where they would play eight games in seven days to determine who would claim the division crown. The Rays needed a spark, and they got one courtesy of this player who batted .455 (10 for 22) with a double, triple, four home runs, seven RBIs, four multi-hit games, a .500 on-base percentage, and a 1.136 slugging percentage for the week. He also hit a game-winning home run vs. Detroit in the 11th inning of the season finale. Who made sure Tampa went into its first postseason as Division Champs by swinging a big stick during the final week of 2008?

   a) Ben Zobrist
   b) Carlos Peña
   c) Evan Longoria
   d) B.J. Upton

QUESTION 14: This player also got hot at the right time for the Rays, winning Player of the Week honors during the second to last week of the 2008 season. He was 7 for 19 with two doubles, three homers, and 11 RBIs. He even had an instant replay that went in his favor, changing a ground rule double call to a home run during the Rays 11-1 thrashing of the Twins on September 19. Who is this player?

   a) Ben Zobrist
   b) Carlos Peña
   c) Evan Longoria
   d) B.J. Upton

QUESTION 15: The Rays swept a series from the Boston Red Sox for the first time in franchise history after this pitcher tossed a complete game shutout on April 27, 2008, outdueling Red Sox ace Josh Beckett. He'd already earned a victory earlier in the week when he tossed seven strong innings vs. Toronto. In 16 total innings he gave up only eight hits and two earned runs while striking out 12, and for his efforts earned Player of the Week honors for the first time in his career. Who is this pitcher?

   a) James Shields
   b) Andy Sonnanstine
   c) Matt Garza
   d) Edwin Jackson

QUESTION 16: In 1998, Tampa's first All-Star was a pitcher (see question #106). The following season the club earned two spots on the All-Star roster—one was Roberto Hernández, who was second in the league with 43 saves, and the other was this powerful hitter who led the team with 34 home runs. Who is this All-Star?
- a) Fred McGriff
- b) Bubba Trammell
- c) Paul Sorrento
- d) Jose Canseco

QUESTION 17: In 2000, Tampa placed an infielder on the All-Star roster for the first time. Who is this All-Star?
- a) John Flaherty
- b) Fred McGriff
- c) Miguel Cairo
- d) Vinny Castilla

QUESTION 18: In 2009, a member of the Rays earned MVP honors during the Mid-Summer Classic for the first time in franchise history. Who is this All-Star MVP?
- a) Scott Kazmir
- b) Jason Bartlett
- c) Carl Crawford
- d) Dioner Navarro

QUESTION 19: And speaking of the 2009 All-Star Game ... the Rays sent *five* players to St. Louis, easily the most in franchise history to make the All-Star team in any one season. Can you identify which five players were All-Stars in 2009?
- a) Carl Crawford, Scott Kazmir, Evan Longoria, Dioner Navarro, Carlos Peña
- b) Carl Crawford, Jason Bartlett, Evan Longoria, Carlos Peña, B.J. Upton
- c) Scott Kazmir, James Shields, Akinori Iwamura, Carl Crawford, Evan Longoria
- d) Jason Bartlett, Carl Crawford, Evan Longoria, Carlos Peña, Ben Zobrist

QUESTION 20: One more with the All-Stars ... do you know which Rays' player was the first in franchise history to be voted a starter on the All-Star team?

    a) Randy Winn
    b) Carl Crawford
    c) Evan Longoria
    d) Ben Zobrist

BOTTOM OF THE FIRST ANSWER KEY

___ QUESTION 11: D
___ QUESTION 12: C*
___ QUESTION 13: A
___ QUESTION 14: B
___ QUESTION 15: A
___ QUESTION 16: D
___ QUESTION 17: B
___ QUESTION 18: C*
___ QUESTION 19: D
___ QUESTION 20: C*

KEEP A RUNNING TALLY OF YOUR CORRECT ANSWERS!

Number correct: ___ / 10

Overall correct: ___ / 20

#12 – Longoria's monster numbers came in June 2008.

#18 – Crawford was 1 for 3 at the plate after entering the game in the fifth inning—but it was his catch in left field, robbing Colorado outfielder Brad Hawpe of a home run, that earned him MVP honors. The A.L. won the game 4-3 at Busch Stadium in St. Louis, thanks to Crawford's catch.

#20 – Longoria won the fan vote to be the starting third baseman in the 2009 All-Star Game, but he ended up sitting out the game due to injury.

Second

AS AN EXPANSION team in its first season, the Rays brought in Hall of Famers Ted Williams, Stan Musial, Al Lopez, and Monte Irvin to throw out ceremonial first pitches before the March 31, 1998, inaugural game vs. the Detroit Tigers.

It's not like a franchise in its first year has its own stock of legends to draw upon ... but it didn't take long for the Rays to make history and to begin the process of acquiring its own legends. In fact, one of Major League Baseball's most recognizable and enduring moments is also one of the first noteworthy achievements by a member of the Tampa Bay ~~Devil~~ Rays: Hall of Fame legend Wade Boggs got his 3,000th career hit on August 7, 1999, as a member of the Rays. Oh, and it was also a home run ...

The first and so far only time in history that a player has reached the 3,000 hit plateau with a bomb, it's a touch ironic that Boggs hit only two homers all season and just 118 throughout his legendary career. Irony aside, it's just downright cool that he did it as a member of the Rays. Boggs went to high school in Tampa, and after giving his best years to the Red Sox and Yankees, winning batting titles and a world championship, he brought his legendary name and status to help the Rays organization get started—and for that, and for the privilege of seeing him make history at The Trop, Rays' fans will always be grateful.

And now back to the questions ... here in the Second, some spectacular performances from guys like Longo, Los, Aki, Huff, and many more ...

TOP OF THE SECOND

QUESTION 21: It's an achievement to lead your team in a significant offensive category, harder still to lead your league, but … to lead all of baseball? Now that's impressive. In 2010 this Rays' All-Star set the Major League standard in four-hit games with eight. It's worth repeating: he had *eight games* in which he had *four hits*. Who is this offensive leader?

    a)   Carl Crawford
    b)   Evan Longoria
    c)   Sean Rodriguez
    d)   Ben Zobrist

QUESTION 22: You might say the Boston Red Sox were responsible for this player earning Player of the Week honors not once, but twice in a span of five weeks. Tampa opened 2009 at Fenway Park and won two of three from the Red Sox—with the spark coming from this player, who was 6 for 14 with two homers and five RBIs in the series. For the week he batted .481 with four doubles, five homers, ten RBIs, 13 hits, and a Major League best 1.185 slugging percentage during Tampa's first six games. A month later the Rays took three out of four from Boston at Tropicana Field—led once more by this same player, who was 7 for 19 with two homers and ten RBIs (including a grand slam) against the Red Sox. Who won Player of the Week honors twice in 2009 courtesy of the Boston Red Sox?

    a)   Carlos Peña
    b)   Pat Burrell
    c)   Evan Longoria
    d)   B.J. Upton

QUESTION 23: When the club began its inaugural season in 1998, whoever led the team in batting was obviously going in the record book … right? I mean, the first to lead the team in batting and, at least temporarily, the highest season average in team history (albeit, a very short history). Well, he did hit .292 that year. Who was Tampa's leading hitter in 1998?

    a)   Quinton McCracken
    b)   Fred McGriff

    c)   Wade Boggs
    d)   Randy Winn

QUESTION 24: The player who led the club in batting that first season will always keep that distinction, and it's a pretty cool one if you think about it—but he's long since been replaced for the highest season average in franchise history. In fact, he held the record for only one season. Who set the new standard for the Rays when he batted .310 in 1999?
    a)   Quinton McCracken
    b)   Fred McGriff
    c)   Wade Boggs
    d)   Randy Winn

QUESTION 25: It's worth noting that in 1998, utility infielder Aaron Ledesma actually batted .324—the only problem is he only had 315 plate appearances, therefore his average doesn't qualify to rank among the team leaders. If he'd maintained that average and accumulated enough plate appearances (502) to qualify, then his would be the best season average in franchise history. Instead that honor belongs to this player, who set a new franchise record when he batted .320 for a season. Not only that, but he also set a franchise record that same year by batting .386 with runners in scoring position. His .320 average was seventh best in the league. Who set this new standard for batting?
    a)   Carl Crawford
    b)   Jason Bartlett
    c)   Wade Boggs
    d)   Aubrey Huff

QUESTION 26: Staying with team records ... through 2010, three players have topped .400 in on-base percentage for Tampa. The franchise record is .411, which was fifth highest in the league that season. So ... who holds the franchise record .411 on-base percentage?

a) Carlos Peña
b) Fred McGriff
c) Jason Bartlett
d) B.J. Upton

QUESTION 27: How about a franchise first ... when Tampa beat the Chicago White Sox on October 2, 2008, during the first postseason game in franchise history, who was on the mound to close out the game and earn the first-ever postseason save for Tampa Bay?
a) Grant Balfour
b) Dan Wheeler
c) J.P. Howell
d) Chad Bradford

QUESTION 28: It's hard to be a playoff contender if your team is weak on defense. In 2008 the Rays made the postseason with a defensive unit that was among the best in the league. In 2009 the Rays' defensive unit was statistically among the worst in the league—and the club missed the playoffs. Then in 2010, Tampa's defense was second best in the league—and earned another trip to the postseason. You just cannot overstate the importance of a solid defensive unit. With that in mind, who was the first player in franchise history to win a Gold Glove Award?
a) Fred McGriff
b) Carlos Peña
c) Dave Martinez
d) Kevin Stocker

QUESTION 29: To follow-up on defense ... can you name the first player in franchise history to win *two* Gold Glove Awards?
a) Fred McGriff
b) Carlos Peña
c) Evan Longoria
d) Dave Martinez

QUESTION 30: Here's another franchise first, also from Tampa's 6-4 win vs. Chicago during Game 1 of the 2008 Division Series. Who was the first player in franchise history to get a hit in the postseason?

    a)   Akinori Iwamura
    b)   B.J. Upton
    c)   Carl Crawford
    d)   Evan Longoria

TOP OF THE SECOND ANSWER KEY

___ QUESTION 21: A
___ QUESTION 22: C*
___ QUESTION 23: A
___ QUESTION 24: B
___ QUESTION 25: B*
___ QUESTION 26: A*
___ QUESTION 27: B
___ QUESTION 28: B*
___ QUESTION 29: C*
___ QUESTION 30: D

KEEP A RUNNING TALLY OF YOUR CORRECT ANSWERS!

Number correct: ___ / 10

Overall correct: ___ / 30

#22 – Longo wasn't the only one punishing Boston during the first week of May. Carlos Peña hit three homers that week and Carl Crawford stole 11 bases. Peña's home runs gave him a Major League best 11 on the season, while Crawford's steals gave him a Major League best 17.

#25 – Bartlett led the team with a .320 average in 2009. Crawford holds three of the top ten season averages in franchise history, Huff holds two of the top ten, Boggs ... none.

#26 – Peña set the standard in 2007.

#28 – Peña won the award in 2008.

#29 – Longo won in back-to-back seasons, 2009-10.

BOTTOM OF THE SECOND

QUESTION 31: The franchise record for hits in a season is 198—good for fifth best in the league that season, and also good for a team high .311 average that was ninth in the league's batting title race. A fifth-round draft pick by Tampa out of the University of Miami—do you know who he is?
   a) Aubrey Huff
   b) Delmon Young
   c) Carl Crawford
   d) Rocco Baldelli

QUESTION 32: After 13 seasons from 1998-2010, only five names appear on the franchise top ten list for most hits in a season—Carl Crawford's name appears on that list six times, and he left for Boston after 2010 as the team's all-time hits leader with 1,480. Aubrey Huff, Delmon Young, and Rocco Baldelli are also on that list. Who is currently tenth on that list, having banged out 182 hits during the 2005 season?
   a) Jorge Cantú
   b) Travis Lee
   c) Alex Gonzalez
   d) Julio Lugo

QUESTION 33: Also in 2005, one of these players set a franchise record for pinch-hits in a season with ten. Do you know which one?
   a) Jorge Cantú
   b) Travis Lee
   c) Alex Gonzalez
   d) Julio Lugo

QUESTION 34: In 13 seasons from 1998-2010, only two Tampa players have scored 100 runs in a season—Carl Crawford has done it three times, including a franchise record 110 runs in 2010. Who is the only other player in franchise history to score 100 runs in a season?

a) B.J. Upton
b) Evan Longoria
c) Aubrey Huff
d) Fred McGriff

QUESTION 35: Carl Crawford hit a franchise record 105 triples during his tenure with the Rays, including a season record 19 in 2004. Crawford owns seven of the top ten season totals for triples in franchise history—including five seasons of ten or more. Who is the only other player in franchise history to hit ten triples in a single season?

a) B.J. Upton
b) Akinori Iwamura
c) Randy Winn
d) Ben Zobrist

QUESTION 36: Only once in franchise history has a member of the Rays led the league in home runs. That same player is also the only one in franchise history to post three seasons of 30 or more homers. Who is this slugger?

a) Evan Longoria
b) Carlos Peña
c) Jose Canseco
d) Aubrey Huff

QUESTION 37: Here's an oddity you might not expect ... only once in 13 seasons of play has a Rays' player managed to work 100 walks in a season—103 to be exact. Who holds the franchise record for most walks in a season?

a) Ben Zobrist
b) Fred McGriff
c) Wade Boggs
d) Carlos Peña

QUESTION 38: With a minimum of 1,500 career plate appearances ... who holds the franchise record with a .296 career batting average?
   a)   Aubrey Huff
   b)   Carl Crawford
   c)   Randy Winn
   d)   Evan Longoria

QUESTION 39: Although it was only second best in the league, this player led the team and set a franchise single-season record when he posted an impressive .627 slugging percentage. Who is this bomber?
   a)   Fred McGriff
   b)   Greg Vaughn
   c)   Jose Canseco
   d)   Carlos Peña

QUESTION 40: With a minimum of 1,500 career plate appearances ... who holds the franchise record with a .380 career on-base percentage?
   a)   Carl Crawford
   b)   Akinori Iwamura
   c)   Fred McGriff
   d)   Carlos Pena

BOTTOM OF THE SECOND ANSWER KEY

___ **QUESTION 31:** A*
___ **QUESTION 32:** D
___ **QUESTION 33:** B
___ **QUESTION 34:** B*
___ **QUESTION 35:** B*
___ **QUESTION 36:** B*
___ **QUESTION 37:** D
___ **QUESTION 38:** B
___ **QUESTION 39:** D*
___ **QUESTION 40:** C

KEEP A RUNNING TALLY OF YOUR CORRECT ANSWERS!

Number correct: ___ / 10

Overall correct: ___ / 40

#31 – Huff set this record in 2003.

#34 – Longo scored exactly 100 to lead the team in 2009.

#35 – Aki hit ten triples in 2007, which was second in the league, but the highest on the team—one more than Crawford's nine.

#36 – Peña led the league with 39 in 2009.

#39 – Peña set this record in 2007.

Third

THE CRIME DOG was the first power threat in the Rays' lineup. Fred McGriff batted cleanup during the first four Opening Day games in Rays' history. Assuming Evan Longoria hits cleanup to open the 2011 campaign, he'll be the first player since McGriff to do so on Opening Day in consecutive seasons. There have been other players to hit cleanup for the Rays multiple times on Opening Day, of course, but none have done so in consecutive seasons, let alone four straight.

McGriff led the Rays in home runs only once, when he hit 19 during Tampa's inaugural season—but after hitting 99 bombs from 1998-2001, he left Tampa as the franchise leader. He was, in fact, the franchise leader in home runs from 1998-2005, until Aubrey Huff became the first player in franchise history to reach 100 career homers on April 18, 2005.

And when it comes to power … Huff was the Rays' first homegrown threat. McGriff was the Tampa native, but it was Huff who was drafted and came up through the Rays' farm system—and who also batted cleanup on Opening Day for the Rays, twice (2004, 2006).

Of course, not every slugger signed by the Rays panned out. The classic example comes from the 2000 season—but you need to go back to 1999 to get the full picture. The Rays acquired high profile slugger Jose Canseco and his nearly 400 career home runs to go along with McGriff. Canseco was on fire, too, blasting home runs left and right until an injury sidelined him for most of the season's second half—and yet he still finished with 34, to go along with McGriff's 32.

And then the Rays added Vinny Castilla and Greg Vaughn for 2000.

Instant optimism, a fan-base full of hope for the first time … a lineup with McGriff, Canseco,

Castilla, and Vaughn, *who wouldn't be excited about that?*

Castilla got tens of millions of dollars from the Rays after hitting nearly 200 home runs in a span of five seasons for the Rockies ... and Vaughn had just come off back-to-back seasons in which he'd hit 50 and 45 home runs respectively.

So what happened in 2000?

McGriff (27) and Vaughn (28) came through ... but Canseco (9) and Castilla (6), eh, not so much.

By the end of 2001, McGriff, Canseco, and Castilla were gone and a valuable lesson had been learned: build from within.

And the Rays began doing that better than any other team in baseball. Okay, so all those top draft picks that came as a result of losing so many games helped ... but it was those same picks who later led the Rays to the postseason, and it's there that we begin our questions in the Third, followed by some franchise records in the bottom of the frame.

TOP OF THE THIRD

QUESTION 41: It took 11 seasons for the Rays to post a winning record. After ten years of futility, Tampa finally earned a postseason berth in 2008 on the strength of the best home record in baseball. Obviously the Rays also set a number of franchise records for wins that season, to include: eight home series sweeps, ten series sweeps, 34 series victories, and most road wins, home wins, and total wins in a season. What was the Rays' MLB best home record in 2008?

    a)   57-24
    b)   56-25
    c)   55-26
    d)   54-27

QUESTION 42: The first postseason game in franchise history was at home vs. the Chicago White Sox on

October 2, 2008. Tampa won 6-4, led by this player, who became just the ninth in MLB history to hit two home runs in his first career postseason game. Not only that, he also homered on the very first postseason pitch he faced and he became just the second player in history to homer during his first two postseason at bats. He later said, "I was nervous. I think if you're not nervous in this situation, you're not really soaking in the moment." Who is this clutch performer?

    a) Carlos Peña
    b) Carl Crawford
    c) B.J. Upton
    d) Evan Longoria

QUESTION 43: To follow-up on the Rays' first playoff game ... this starter gave up just six hits before leaving with a 6-3 lead in the seventh. Who took the mound and earned the win during the first playoff game in franchise history?

    a) Scott Kazmir
    b) James Shields
    c) Matt Garza
    d) Andy Sonnanstine

QUESTION 44: Tampa clinched the Division Series vs. Chicago with a 6-2 victory on the road at U.S. Cellular Field in Game 4, thanks in large part to yet another strong outing by its starting pitcher. Afterwards, White Sox manager Ozzie Guillen said, "They played better than us. There's no doubt. They pitched better. They executed better. They got big hits. They really did a tremendous job." The victory made Tampa just the fifth team during the expansion era (since 1961) to win its first postseason series. Who started and earned the victory that clinched the Rays' first-ever postseason series?

    a) Scott Kazmir
    b) James Shields

c)   Matt Garza
d)   Andy Sonnanstine

QUESTION 45: After eliminating Chicago, the Rays moved on to face the Boston Red Sox in the American League Championship Series. This player said, "It means everything. We've been at the bottom of the barrel for so long, I think there was a point in time where people didn't even know who we were." Well, after his performance against Chicago and Boston, he made sure people know not only who the Rays are, but who he is, as well. He hit two home runs in the clinching game vs. Chicago, and in the two series' he combined for 14 hits, 13 runs, a double, triple, seven home runs, and 15 RBIs ... all this after hitting only *nine* home runs during the regular season. Who came alive at the plate in a big way during the first two rounds of the 2008 postseason?
a)   Willy Aybar
b)   Eric Hinske
c)   B.J. Upton
d)   Gabe Gross

QUESTION 46: Tampa lost Game 1 of the American League Championship Series, 2-0. Daisuke Matsuzaka was dominant for the Red Sox, giving up just four hits in seven-plus innings of work. Dice-K was so good that he carried a no-hitter into the seventh inning. Who broke up the no-hit bid with a leadoff single for the Rays in the bottom of the seventh?
a)   Akinori Iwamura
b)   Carlos Peña
c)   Carl Crawford
d)   Gabe Gross

QUESTION 47: Game 2 of the ALCS vs. Boston was an epic slugfest that ended with a mad dash to the plate in extra-innings. The teams combined for seven home runs, tying a postseason record. Evan Longoria became the third youngest player in MLB history to hit three homers in a single postseason when he went yard against Josh Beckett. B.J. Upton and Cliff Floyd also homered against Beckett, but it was a shallow sacrifice fly off the bat of Upton that won the game 9-8 in the 11th inning when pinch-runner Fernando Perez (who had 43 steals in Class-AAA and was 5 for 5 in stolen bases with the Rays that season) raced to the plate ahead of the throw from right fielder J.D. Drew. Lost in the midst of all that offense was the fact the Rays' bullpen blanked the Red Sox over the final three-plus innings of play. Rookie sensation David Price pitched two-thirds of an inning to earn the win ... but which member of the Rays' bullpen was the real hero, tossing 3.1 innings of one-hit, scoreless relief before yielding to Price in the 11th?

- a) J.P. Howell
- b) Grant Balfour
- c) Chad Bradford
- d) Dan Wheeler

QUESTION 48: Tampa won Game 3 of the ALCS in Boston, and then gave the ball to this pitcher to start Game 4 ... and after giving up a homer to Kevin Cash to start the third all he did was retire 12 straight batters. He carried a two-hitter into the seventh before giving up a triple to David Ortiz. All total he pitched seven-plus solid innings en route to a convincing 13-4 win and a 3-1 lead in the series. Who was the winning pitcher during Game 4 of the 2008 ALCS?

- a) Scott Kazmir
- b) James Shields
- c) Matt Garza
- d) Andy Sonnanstine

QUESTION 49: The Rays 16 home runs vs. Boston during the ALCS set a new record—it took only five games, however, to break the previous record, which was 12. In Game 5, one member of the Rays tied an

ALCS record by hitting a home run in his third consecutive game. Two days later, in Game 6, another member of the Rays tied the same record ... however, just five pitches later, the player who tied the record in Game 5 went yard again, setting a new record with home runs in *four* consecutive ALCS games. In both Game 5 and Game 6 these players hit back-to-back home runs, but do you know which one homered in a record four consecutive games?

    a) Carlos Peña
    b) B.J. Upton
    c) Evan Longoria
    d) Willy Aybar

QUESTION 50: Tampa took a commanding 3-1 lead in the series before losing Game 5 in heartbreaking fashion. The Rays led 7-0 as Game 5 moved into the home half of the seventh—but a four-run seventh followed by a three-run eighth led to a walk-off win for the Red Sox in the ninth, 8-7. Boston went on to win Game 6 in Tampa, 4-2, and suddenly it was down to a do-or-die Game 7. No worries ... Tampa gave the ball to this starter, who struck out nine while giving up just two hits in seven-plus innings, as the Rays clinched the Pennant with a 3-1 victory. He was 2-0 in the series with a 1.38 earned run average and he earned series MVP honors. Who is this clutch pitcher?

    a) Scott Kazmir
    b) James Shields
    c) Matt Garza
    d) Andy Sonnanstine

TOP OF THE THIRD ANSWER KEY

___ QUESTION 41: A*
___ QUESTION 42: D
___ QUESTION 43: B
___ QUESTION 44: D
___ QUESTION 45: C
___ QUESTION 46: C
___ QUESTION 47: D
___ QUESTION 48: D*
___ QUESTION 49: C*
___ QUESTION 50: C

KEEP A RUNNING TALLY OF YOUR CORRECT ANSWERS!

Number correct: ___ / 10

Overall correct: ___ / 50

#41 – Tampa was 40-41 on the road, good for a franchise best 97 wins on the season.

#48 – Sonnanstine had also pitched 13 scoreless innings in two starts vs. Boston just a month earlier, though in both starts he received a no-decision.

#49 – It was Peña who also homered in three straight ALCS games. Also, Longo and Upton became the first teammates in history with at least six homers apiece in one postseason.

BOTTOM OF THE THIRD

QUESTION 51: Now for some pitching ... one player is on the franchise top ten leader board for earned run average four times, including three consecutive seasons that all rank among the five best in franchise history. Who is this pitcher?

    a)   James Shields
    b)   Scott Kazmir
    c)   Rolando Arrojo
    d)   Tanyon Sturtze

QUESTION 52: In Tampa's inaugural 1998 season the team leader posted a 3.56 earned run average that remained the best season effort for the franchise until 2006. The record fell again in 2010 when one member of the Rays' starting rotation was third in the league with a 2.72 ERA. Who set a new franchise record for ERA in 2010?

    a)   Matt Garza
    b)   James Shields
    c)   Jeff Niemann
    d)   David Price

QUESTION 53: Believe it or not, the team record for wins by a starting pitcher that was established in 1998 was not eclipsed until 2010. In fact, it wasn't until 2008 when both Edwin Jackson and James Shields won 14 games that the initial record was even equaled. Two members of the 2010 Rays' pitching staff bested it, however—including one who was second in the league with 19 wins. In 2010, the Rays actually had five starting pitchers with 12 or more wins ... but which two eclipsed the old team record of 14?

    a)   David Price and Matt Garza
    b)   Matt Garza and James Shields
    c)   David Price and James Shields
    d)   Matt Garza and Jeff Niemann

QUESTION 54: The season record for most strikeouts per nine innings is 10.41. Who set this record for the Rays?
   a)   David Price
   b)   Matt Garza
   c)   Scott Kazmir
   d)   Ryan Rupe

QUESTION 55: In 13 seasons from 1998-2010 only one pitcher has eclipsed 200 strikeouts in a season for the Rays. A few have come close to 200, but the record of 239 is *50* more than the second highest total. Who set this franchise record?
   a)   David Price
   b)   Scott Kazmir
   c)   Tony Saunders
   d)   Matt Garza

QUESTION 56: The franchise record for saves is 45. That record belongs to this player, whose total led the league and earned him both an All-Star appearance and the A.L. Rolaids Relief Award. Who is this reliever?
   a)   Danys Báez
   b)   Roberto Hernández
   c)   Rafael Soriano
   d)   Esteban Yan

QUESTION 57: The franchise record for career saves is 101. That record belongs to a player who never led the league in any given season, although his career high of 43 was second in the league and set the franchise standard for a lot of years. Who is this reliever?
   a)   Roberto Hernández
   b)   Danys Báez
   c)   Esteban Yan
   d)   Alberto Reyes

QUESTION 58: Matt Garza is tied for the most career complete games in franchise history. His grand total ... *six*. James Shields (five) and Jeff Niemann (three) are the closest active players who conceivably can tie or pass that mark in 2011. Oddly enough, the franchise record for most complete games in a season is five ... just one less than the career record. Who owns the franchise record with five complete games in a single season?

    a)   Matt Garza
    b)   Joe Kennedy
    c)   Albie Lopez
    d)   Tanyon Sturtze

QUESTION 59: The franchise record for converting the most consecutive saves is 19. A native Puerto Rican and a former first-round draft pick of the California Angels, who is the stalwart reliever that set this mark?

    a)   Roberto Hernández
    b)   Danys Báez
    c)   Esteban Yan
    d)   Alberto Reyes

QUESTION 60: One more record for the bullpen ... the highest saves percentage in franchise history is 91.5. This reliever failed to convert only four save opportunities on his way to establishing this record. Who is he?

    a)   Roberto Hernández
    b)   Danys Báez
    c)   Esteban Yan
    d)   Alberto Reyes

BOTTOM OF THE THIRD ANSWER KEY

___ QUESTION 51: B*
___ QUESTION 52: D
___ QUESTION 53: A*
___ QUESTION 54: C
___ QUESTION 55: B*
___ QUESTION 56: C*
___ QUESTION 57: A
___ QUESTION 58: B*
___ QUESTION 59: A*
___ QUESTION 60: A*

KEEP A RUNNING TALLY OF YOUR CORRECT ANSWERS!

Number correct: ___ / 10

Overall correct: ___ / 60

#51 – Including three consecutive seasons from 2006-08.

#53 – Price (19), Garza (15); the others with at least 12 wins were Wade Davis (12), Jeff Niemann (12) and James Shields (13).

#55 – Kazmir led the league with 239 strikeouts in 2007.

#56 – All this in 2010.

#58 – Kennedy had five complete games in 2002, second best in the league, but his record was just 8-11. Kennedy is also tied with Garza for the career mark of six complete games.

#59 – His streak of consecutive saves came in 1999.

#60 – Also in 1999.

Andy Sonnanstine

Fourth

THE DRAFT PICKS ... the lifeblood of any organization, its impossible to overstate their importance to an expansion franchise. Tampa first participated in the June Amateur Draft in 1996, selecting a total of 97 players ... which begs several questions: Who was the first player drafted by the Rays? Who was the first to make it to the big leagues? Who went on to have the best career?

Well, Paul Wilder was the Rays' first draft pick. The 29th overall pick, he was an outfielder from Cary High School, in Cary, North Carolina. He played six years in the minors without much success, and never made it to the majors.

The Rays' second pick and the 64th player taken in the draft came out of Buchholz High School just up the road from Tampa, in Gainesville, Florida—and he had tons of success post-high school ... as quarterback for the Florida Gators, that is. Doug Johnson was a two-sport star with one of the best arms in the 1996 Draft, but he was a corner infielder for the Rays and a quarterback for the Gators ... and football won out. Johnson eventually was the backup to Michael Vick for the Atlanta Falcons.

The Rays' third pick and the 124th player taken in the draft also came out of high school, a lefty pitcher named Cedrick Bowers. He was practically Doug Johnson's neighbor, having played ball at Chiefland High School, which is just down the road from Gainesville. Bowers actually made it to the big leagues with the Colorado Rockies ... *in 2008!* Talk about perseverance, the guy has spent parts of eight seasons playing Class-AAA ball (and counting) ... how that happens for a 6' 2" 220 lb lefty we've no idea, but there you go. In 19 Major League games he's 0-1 with a 7.40 earned run average.

Only nine of the 97 players selected by the Rays that first season ever tasted action in the big leagues—and of those nine, for most it was only a cup of coffee. To answer the question of who made it to the big leagues first, well, that was Mickey Callaway, who was selected in the seventh-round and was also the seventh player chosen by the Rays. He debuted for the Rays on June 12, 1999. Callaway came out of college and that put him on a faster track for the big leagues than many of the other draftees. He made four starts and one relief appearance for Tampa just three years after being drafted. It took him another two years to earn a brief return trip to the big club. All total he spent parts of five seasons pitching for three teams at the big league level, but without much success.

So to answer the question of who has been the most successful from among those original 97 players drafted by the Rays ... well, it might surprise you. That's because he's a familiar name, yet many forget he began his career as a Devil Ray. Most only know him as the guy we got for sending Ty Wigginton to the Astros ... yup, that's right: Dan Wheeler.

Drafted by the Rays in the 34th round ... after 1,023 other players were chosen ahead of him. Dan Wheeler is easily the most successful player Tampa selected during its initial June Amateur Draft—both in terms of numbers and longevity. Wheeler debuted not long after Callaway—on September 1, 1999. Only 21 at the time, he struggled to a 0-4 record during his September call-up. Later released by the club, he found success with the Mets and Astros before working his way back to where he started: with the Rays.

In subsequent years, the Rays have drafted very well. Aubrey Huff was the first Rays' draft pick to become a real impact player at the big league level. He was selected in the fifth-round of the 1998 draft. And then of course, there's 1999—Josh Hamilton and Carl Crawford. Hamilton the first overall pick, Crawford in the second round, the 52nd overall pick.

The Rays were right about Hamilton's ability, it's just unfortunate for him that his path to the big leagues took him through some pretty dark places. In 2000, the Rays drafted Rocco Baldelli, James Shields, and Shawn Riggans—not a bad year at all. Jonny Gomes in 2001 ... B.J. Upton in 2002 ... Delmon Young and John Jaso in 2003 ... and talk about a bumper crop, in 2004: Jeff Niemann, Reid Brignac, Wade Davis, Jake McGee, Fernando Perez, and Andy Sonnanstine! Jeremy Hellickson in 2005 ... Evan Longoria and Desmond Jennings in 2006 ... and, of course, David Price, the overall number one pick in 2007.

Worth repeating: draft picks are the lifeblood of any organization. It might have taken a couple years to get the hang of it, but as the 2008 season proved, the Rays have drafted better than most.

Now back to the questions ... here in the Fourth, some franchise firsts and even more extraordinary performances.

TOP OF THE FOURTH

QUESTION 61: In November 1997, Tampa Bay began preparing for its upcoming inaugural season by hiring its first-ever manager. Who did the Rays hire to guide the team that first season—Larry Rothschild or Hal McRae?

QUESTION 62: That same month the Major League Expansion Draft was held in Phoenix, Arizona. Who did the Rays select with the very first pick in the draft—Quinton McCracken or Tony Saunders?

QUESTION 63: The following month tickets went on sale for Opening Day 1998 ... and Tampa's first game sold out in just 17 minutes. Three days later the club made headlines again by landing a huge acquisition via free agency. Who was Tampa's first big free agent signing in December 1997—Wade Boggs or Fred McGriff?

QUESTION 64: In the 1999 June Amateur Draft, the Rays selected outfielder Josh Hamilton with the first overall pick. Hamilton turned out to be every bit as good as advertised, just not during the time he was in the Rays organization. The Rays could have selected an ace pitcher instead of Hamilton, but opted to pick a bat instead of an arm. Who is the ace that was selected second overall behind Josh Hamilton that year—Josh Beckett or Barry Zito?

QUESTION 65: This player made history for Tampa on September 23, 2000, when he hit a home run against Toronto's Roy Halladay. The reason his blast was significant? It was his 200th in the American League, making him just the second player in MLB history to hit 200-plus home runs in both the National and American Leagues. The first player to do so was Hall of Fame legend Frank Robinson. And the second ... was it Greg Vaughn or Fred McGriff?

QUESTION 66: Tampa began 2002 with a three-game sweep of the Detroit Tigers at Tropicana Field for its best start yet in five seasons of play. Unfortunately, by the end of the month the Rays were mired in a franchise worst 15-game losing streak. In the midst of that streak the Rays were also the victims of a no-hitter for the first time. On April 27, 2002, who became the first pitcher to throw a no-hitter vs. Tampa—Derek Lowe or Hideo Nomo?

QUESTION 67: In June 2002, one member of the Rays made history when he became just the 39th player in MLB history to hit two home runs in the same inning ... and he was a rookie! Who pulled off this extraordinary feat—Jared Sandberg or Aubrey Huff?

QUESTION 68: Also in 2002, it was a rookie who led the Rays in home runs, despite not being called up from Class-AAA Durham until May 28. He hit 23 home runs with a .520 slugging percentage to lead the club in both categories—was it Jared Sandberg or Aubrey Huff?

QUESTION 69: After the 2002 season the Rays hired Lou Piniella as the third manager in team history. In order to get Piniella, who is a Tampa native and played for the University of Tampa, the Rays had to give up a player to the Seattle Mariners, seeing as Piniella was the Mariners manager from 1993-2002 and was still under contract. Piniella got a four-year deal worth $13 million ... and the Mariners got which player from the Rays—Randy Winn or Andy Sheets?

QUESTION 70: After beginning 2002 with a sweep of Detroit, the Rays were in for more excitement in April 2003, when one member of the Rays set a MLB record for rookies by collecting 40 hits in the season's first month, surpassing the previous record of 39 set by Ichiro Suzuki in April 2001. Who got his career off to such a hot start—Carl Crawford or Rocco Baldelli?

TOP OF THE FOURTH ANSWER KEY

___ **QUESTION 61:** Larry Rothschild
___ **QUESTION 62:** Tony Saunders
___ **QUESTION 63:** Wade Boggs
___ **QUESTION 64:** Josh Beckett
___ **QUESTION 65:** Fred McGriff
___ **QUESTION 66:** Derek Lowe
___ **QUESTION 67:** Jared Sandberg
___ **QUESTION 68:** Aubrey Huff
___ **QUESTION 69:** Randy Winn
___ **QUESTION 70:** Rocco Baldelli

KEEP A RUNNING TALLY OF YOUR CORRECT ANSWERS!

Number correct: ___ / 10

Overall correct: ___ / 70

BOTTOM OF THE FOURTH

QUESTION 71: In 2004, two American League players hit double digits in RBIs as a pinch-hitter—the Yankees' Ruben Sierra (11) and the Indians' Ben Broussard (10). On September 14, 2010, this member of the Rays hit a three-run pinch-hit home run to give him ten RBIs on the season as a pinch-hitter. It was the first time since 2004 that anyone in the A.L. hit double digits in RBIs coming off the bench. Who did this for the Rays—Willy Aybar or Dan Johnson?

QUESTION 72: At the end of June 2010, one member of the Rays' starting rotation was a dismal 5-9 in 15 starts and he lost all five of his starts in June ... but then he caught fire. He was 6-0 in his next eight starts, including 4-0 in July and 2-0 in August. No other pitcher in baseball had as many as six wins during that span without losing at least one game. Who was unbeatable for the Rays during July and August 2010—Jeff Niemann or Wade Davis?

QUESTION 73: Tampa began play on August 28, 2010, tied with the Yankees for the A.L. East lead, just 4.5 games ahead of the Red Sox. The Yankees beat the White Sox 12-9, so the Rays needed a win vs. Boston to stay tied for the division lead and gain some separation from the Red Sox. The pitching match-up: Clay Buchholz vs. Matt Garza. Both starters were dominant—Buchholz pitched into the eighth, allowing just four hits and one earned run, while Garza gave up just six hits and one earned run in seven innings of work—but neither figured in the decision as the game moved to extra-innings. And that's when this player called a team meeting at home plate in the home half of the tenth ... translation: he hit a walk-off home run, the first of his career. Whose dramatic walk-off home run to beat Boston allowed the Rays to keep pace with the Yankees in the A.L. East race—Willy Aybar or Dan Johnson?

QUESTION 74: To follow-up on that last question ... Clay Buchholz extended an impressive streak to 30.1 innings without allowing an earned run. That is, until this Rays' player hit a game-tying home run in the eighth inning, which set the stage for the walk-off heroics in the tenth. It was his 13th homer of the season. Who hit this clutch shot—Ben Zobrist or B.J. Upton?

QUESTION 75: And speaking of clutch ... in baseball statistics a late-inning pressure situation is defined as any plate appearance in the seventh inning or later in which the score is tied, the team at bat is trailing by three or fewer runs, or the team at bat is trailing by four runs but has at least two runners on base. Tampa beat Oakland 5-4 on August 21, 2010, after trailing 4-2 in the top of the eighth inning. In the eighth, Willy Aybar hit an RBI double to make it 4-2, and then this player delivered a two-run home run that proved to be the game-winner. For Aybar it was his 12th hit of the season during a late-inning pressure situation—good for a .343 average that at the time was second best in the league. And the only guy with a higher average (.344) in those situations was, well ... the same teammate that hit the game-winning home run. Who was he—Sean Rodriguez or Evan Longoria?

QUESTION 76: A Rays' rookie accomplished a franchise first in historic fashion in 2010—he won his first three Major League starts. And not only that, but he was the first pitcher in baseball's modern era (since 1900!) to pitch six-plus innings while giving up three or fewer hits during his first three starts. Now that's pretty impressive. Who began his career in such an extraordinary way—Jeremy Hellickson or Jake McGee?

QUESTION 77: In 1999, Rays' catcher John Flaherty hit two home runs in a 13-3 road thrashing of the Texas Rangers on May 17. Four months later, Texas visited

The Trop and Flaherty did it again—blasting two more long balls vs. the Rangers on September 17 as the Rays won 7-5. Until 2010, those two games were the only ones in franchise history in which a Rays' catcher had a multi-homer game. Every other team in baseball had at least two multi-homer games by catchers during the intervening years, but not the Rays ... not until this catcher hit a solo blast and a grand slam to beat the Orioles 7-3 on August 14, 2010. Who was it—John Jaso or Kelly Shoppach?

QUESTION 78: Tampa beat Minnesota 6-4 on August 3, 2010. It was a significant victory for a couple of reasons: one, it moved the Rays into solo first place in the A.L. East, and two, it was the tenth victory of the season for one of Tampa's starting pitchers. Not only that, but this starter was the fourth member of the Rays' rotation to earn his tenth win—and the team had only played 106 games! It was only the third time in the past four decades that a Major League team had four pitchers, all of whom were in their 20s, reach double digits in wins that early in a season. The Mets did it in 1986 with Dwight Gooden, Ron Darling, Sid Fernandez, and Bob Ojeda. The Phillies did it in 2003 with Kevin Millwood, Vicente Padilla, Randy Wolf, and Brett Myers. The Rays did it with David Price, Jeff Niemann, Matt Garza, and James Shields. Which one of those starters was the fourth man in the rotation to hit double digits in wins in 2010—Price, Niemann, Garza, or Shields?

QUESTION 79: Matt Garza and Max Scherzer were locked in an epic pitching duel on July 26, 2010. Garza and the Rays prevailed vs. the Tigers 5-0 as he tossed the first no-hitter in franchise history and faced the minimum 27 batters—but Scherzer didn't allow a hit until the sixth inning. Oh, but what a hit it was ... the first of the ballgame, it was a grand slam. It was the first time in 20 years that a no-hit game was broken up in the sixth inning or later by a grand slam. Whose bases loaded jack gave Garza all the support he needed to win his no-hit gem vs. the Tigers—Sean Rodriguez or Matt Joyce?

QUESTION 80: On July 24, 2010, David Price took the mound for the Rays with a 12-5 record and a 2.84 earned run average. His opponent that day: 8-8 with a 3.89 ERA. Advantage Tampa, right? Not so fast. The Rays fell behind early, 3-0. And worse, coming into the game Tampa had lost *18 consecutive games* against this team on the road, where this game was being played. Maybe the 2000 version of the Devil Rays ... but not the 2010 Rays, doesn't sound possible, does it? And yet, very true. Fortunately on this day, Ben Zobrist hit a three-run home run and the Rays rallied for a 6-3 victory. It was the Rays' fifth road win of the season in a game in which they had trailed by at least three runs—which was the highest total in the majors at the time. It also brought to an end this long and surprising road losing streak to which team—the Cleveland Indians or the Chicago White Sox?

BOTTOM OF THE FOURTH ANSWER KEY

___ **QUESTION 71:** Willy Aybar
___ **QUESTION 72:** Wade Davis
___ **QUESTION 73:** Dan Johnson
___ **QUESTION 74:** B.J. Upton
___ **QUESTION 75:** Sean Rodriguez
___ **QUESTION 76:** Jeremy Hellickson
___ **QUESTION 77:** Kelly Shoppach
___ **QUESTION 78:** Jeff Niemann
___ **QUESTION 79:** Matt Joyce
___ **QUESTION 80:** Cleveland Indians

KEEP A RUNNING TALLY OF YOUR CORRECT ANSWERS!

Number correct: ___ / 10

Overall correct: ___ / 80

Joe Maddon and a young Rays fan – courtesy author.

Fifth

NINE EQUALS EIGHT ... just ask any math teacher. Well, make that a Tampa-St. Pete area math teacher, one who also likes baseball, and is a diehard Rays fan, and who knows that Joe Maddon deserves more than just the 2008 Manager of the Year Award, he deserves ... well, a place in the Hall of Fame might be overstating things a touch, but not by much.

It's pretty simple, actually—the Rays had never won more than 70 games in a season. Ten seasons, 645 wins ... 972 losses. Joe Maddon had just managed the previous two seasons for the club, having won 61 and 66 games respectively. And yet, he showed up in Spring Training 2008 with this philosophy: 9=8.

He made tee shirts that said: 9=8.

He put signs around the clubhouse.

He preached it.

He believed it.

And soon, so did the players.

And later, so did everyone else.

Nine players playing as one unit equals one of eight teams going to the playoffs.

Hey, 97 regular season wins, a Division Series victory, and one Pennant later ... the math really does work, right?

Later, Maddon got the chance to laugh about his math—which he could do, seeing as he was basking in the glow of that big trophy they give you when you win the American League Championship Series. But even *before* beating the Red Sox in Game 7 of the 2008 ALCS, Maddon had this to say during a pregame interview: "Let's go back to the first day of Spring Training. If I had told you guys we were going to be one game away from going to the World Series, all of you would have laughed. Absolutely, a good belly-laugh. I'm very proud of where our group is at today, and I could understand why you would have belly-laughed back then. But nobody is laughing right now. And I could not be more proud of this group, and I have a strong conviction and belief that we're going to get it done tonight."

And sure enough, the Rays got it done.

After winning the Pennant, James Shields said, "When he brought out this 9=8 thing, we kind of all looked at each other like, 'What's this guy talking about?' And it made sense in the end. We believed in it, and we believed in ourselves. I think that's kind of what the point of all his slogans talk about—you've got to believe in yourselves before anybody else does."

Which explains something else Maddon did— he hung a sign written in English, Spanish, Japanese, and Korean, and it read: "Attitude is a decision."

Thanks to Maddon, the Rays made a simple yet profound decision in 2008: they believed they could win.

Cliff Floyd said, "Once we got a hold of this thing and started to believe, we became a family that you couldn't defeat. And here we are."

Here we are, indeed. A Pennant and two Division Titles in three years, a force to be reckoned with in the most vicious division in baseball, all because a manager believed he could change the rules of math ... and he was *right*.

On to the Fifth, where plenty of good pitching and timely hitting awaits ... but can you match the names with these amazing performances?

TOP OF THE FIFTH

QUESTION 81: In 2005, the St. Louis Cardinals won Chris Carpenter's first nine road starts of the season. It wasn't until 2010 that a Major League club began the season with a streak that long, when the Rays won nine consecutive road starts by this pitcher to begin the season. Who is he?

a) David Price
b) Jeff Niemann
c) Matt Garza
d) James Shields

QUESTION 82: Yankee Stadium is a tough stop on a road trip whether you're a rookie or a veteran, but it's notoriously tough on rookies. In fact, since the original Yankee Stadium opened in 1923 there have only been three rookies in Major League history who can boast having hit two home runs with five RBIs in a single road game in the Bronx: Harry Davis did it for Detroit in 1932, Jason Varitek did it for Boston in 1998, and ... this rookie, who did it on July 17, 2010, in a 10-5 Rays' victory.

a) Desmond Jennings
b) Reid Brignac
c) John Jaso
d) Sean Rodriguez

QUESTION 83: Five different members of the Rays' pitching staff recorded a save in 2010—four of which were fulltime members of the bullpen, although one, Andy Sonnanstine, also made four starts. The fifth player who earned a save, however, was an integral part of the Rays' starting rotation. On July 7, Manager Joe Maddon used him out of the bullpen to earn a save in the finale of a three-game sweep of the Boston Red Sox because closer Rafael Soriano was unavailable after saving five games in the previous six days. Just three days later, this same starter pitched one-hit ball over six shutout innings in a 4-0 victory vs. Cleveland. Not a bad week's work ... in fact, he was the first MLB player in four years to earn a save and win a game as a starter during the same week. Who was this pitcher willing to take the ball in any situation for Manager Joe Maddon?

a) David Price
b) Jeff Niemann

c) Matt Garza
d) James Shields

QUESTION 84: In the "tough save" category ... this Rays' pitcher earned the first save of his career in spectacular fashion on June 19, 2010. The day before, the Marlins roughed up Matt Garza for five runs in the first and two more in the second, forcing Joe Maddon to go to his bullpen very early. He called on this pitcher, who came in and tossed shutout ball for 4.1 innings, throwing 55 pitches. And then on June 19, after using eight pitchers in ten-plus innings, Maddon was forced to call on him again after the Marlins put the potential tying and go-ahead runners on first and third with no outs in the 11th. How did he respond? Back-to-back strikeouts and a fly out to end the game and preserve a 9-8 Rays' victory— making him the first pitcher in a decade to earn a save the day after throwing at least 50 pitches in another game. Who is this Rays' workhorse?
a) Lance Cormier
b) Joaquin Benoit
c) Andy Sonnanstine
d) Jeremy Hellickson

QUESTION 85: The Florida Marlins beat Tampa Bay 6-1 on June 13, 2010, to deal Jeff Niemann his first loss of the season. Niemann had been 6-0 through his first 12 starts, but he fell one shy of the franchise record for undefeated starts at the beginning of a season, which is 13. Who set this franchise record when he began a season 6-0 through 13 starts?
a) Scott Kazmir
b) Matt Garza
c) James Shields
d) David Price

QUESTION 86: As the Marlins put an end to Niemann's win streak, Evan Longoria used that same series to extend a streak of his own. On June 12, Longo hit an RBI single vs. Ricky Nolasco to become just the third player in franchise history to reach base safely in 30 consecutive games. In 2008, Carlos Peña also reached base safely in 30 consecutive games—but which of the following players set the franchise record of 37 consecutive games in 2001?

    a)   Ben Grieve
    b)   Randy Winn
    c)   Fred McGriff
    d)   Jason Tyner

QUESTION 87: On June 6, 2010, the Rays' leadoff man was 3 for 5 with two runs, a homer, and five RBIs in a 9-5 victory on the road vs. Texas. It was the first time in franchise history that a player batting leadoff had more than four RBIs in one game. Who accomplished this franchise first?

    a)   Carl Crawford
    b)   B.J. Upton
    c)   Jason Bartlett
    d)   John Jaso

QUESTION 88: And speaking of leadoff men posting crazy numbers ... in 2003, in a span of five games between the Yankees and Rays played at Tropicana Field, Alfonso Soriano led off three of them with a home run for the Yanks. No other player in baseball hit three leadoff homers on the road, against the same opponent, in five or fewer games, until 2009-10 ... when this member of the Rays returned the favor and hit three leadoff homers in a span of five games at Yankee Stadium. Which leadoff man did this amazing feat?

    a)   Carl Crawford
    b)   B.J. Upton
    c)   Jason Bartlett
    d)   John Jaso

QUESTION 89: On April 19, 2010, Tampa completed a sweep of a four-game series on the road in a hostile environment. How hostile? Well, consider this: since 2000, this team had a home record of 80-34 for games played during the season's first month. With a .702 winning percentage, that was easily the best record in baseball during that time span. In fact, the last time this team was swept in a four-game series at home during April was back in 1996. Which team did the Rays send reeling early in 2010?

    a)   New York Yankees
    b)   Boston Red Sox
    c)   Anaheim Angels
    d)   Detroit Tigers

QUESTION 90: Matt Garza got off to a fast start in 2010, winning his first three starts—two against Baltimore, and his third on the road at Fenway. It was only the third time in franchise history that a Rays' pitcher won the first three games he pitched in a season. The first player to do so was Doug Waechter, who won the first three games of his big league career when he was a 22-year-old rookie with Tampa in 2003—however, one of Waechter's wins came as a reliever. The first time a Rays' pitcher earned a win in his first three starts of a season was 2004. Who got off to such a hot start in 2004?

    a)   Victor Zambrano
    b)   Mark Hendrickson
    c)   Rob Bell
    d)   Jorge Sosa

TOP OF THE FIFTH ANSWER KEY

___ QUESTION 81: B
___ QUESTION 82: B
___ QUESTION 83: C
___ QUESTION 84: C
___ QUESTION 85: C*
___ QUESTION 86: A
___ QUESTION 87: D*
___ QUESTION 88: C*
___ QUESTION 89: B
___ QUESTION 90: A

KEEP A RUNNING TALLY OF YOUR CORRECT ANSWERS!

Number correct: ___ / 10

Overall correct: ___ / 90

#85 – Shields did it in 2007.

#87 – What really stands out here is that Jaso is, of course, a catcher. He was, however, the DH in this particular game.

#88 – Not five consecutive games calendar-wise. The first was on May 7, 2009, against Andy Pettitte, the second was on September 9, 2009, against Joba Chamberlain, and the third was on May 19, 2010, against A.J. Burnett—there were two other games in that span that Bartlett batted leadoff at Yankee Stadium, and in one of them he actually hit another home run, but it wasn't leading off the game.

BOTTOM OF THE FIFTH

QUESTION 91: Talk about clutch ... this player hit a three-run homer in the top of the tenth to lead the Rays to victory, 8-6, vs. the Baltimore Orioles on April 13, 2010. The very next day he blasted a three-run homer in the first inning to pace the Rays to a 9-1 victory vs. the Orioles. And with those two blasts, he became the first player in franchise history to hit a three-run homer in consecutive innings—the tenth inning on April 13, and the first inning on April 14. Who is this clutch hitter?

    a) Evan Longoria
    b) Carl Crawford
    c) Carlos Peña
    d) Ben Zobrist

QUESTION 92: And continuing the clutch theme ... on Opening Day 2010, this player hit a two-run double in the bottom of the ninth to give the Rays a 4-3 walk-off win vs. the Orioles. This same player had previously hit a walk-off homer in an Opening Day game for the Rays—and with his walk-off hit in 2010 he became the first player in four decades to win multiple Opening Day games in walk-off fashion. Who is this clutch hitter?

    a) Evan Longoria
    b) Carl Crawford
    c) Carlos Peña
    d) Ben Zobrist

QUESTION 93: In 2009, this pitcher was 17-10 after winning 20 games in 2008. He pretty much dominated the American League ... but not the Rays. Four of his ten losses in 2009 were against Tampa, two each to Jeff Niemann and David Price. This pitcher was 32-14 against the rest of the league in 2008-09, but only 3-7 vs. the Rays. Who is this ace that had nothing but trouble against the Rays?

a) Jon Lester
b) Cliff Lee
c) Roy Halladay
d) Josh Beckett

QUESTION 94: On July 25, 1992, a pitcher named Tim Fortugno won his first Major League game. Pitching for the Angels, he tossed a three-hit shutout vs. the Detroit Tigers and struck out 12 batters. It took another 17 years before another big league pitcher tossed a shutout with at least ten strikeouts for his first big league win ... and he did it for the Rays in 2009. Whose first big league victory came in such spectacular fashion?

a) Jeff Niemann
b) David Price
c) Wade Davis
d) Winston Abreu

QUESTION 95: Ben Zobrist, Gabe Gross, and Carlos Peña all homered to back a strong pitching effort from winner Andy Sonnanstine as the Rays won an interleague match-up vs. the Washington Nationals 8-3 on June 13, 2009. The home run for Peña was especially significant as it was his 20th of the season despite the fact the Rays had played only 64 games. That's the second fastest in franchise history that a player has reached 20 homers in a season. The franchise record is 53 games—do you know who started a season on such a prodigious pace for the Rays?

a) Fred McGriff
b) Greg Vaughn
c) Jose Canseco
d) Aubrey Huff

QUESTION 96: Matt Garza pitched one of the Rays' best games of the season on August 15, 2008. It was a complete game shutout on the road vs. the Texas

Rangers. Garza gave up just two hits and two walks while striking out nine. It was also his tenth win of the season, which for the first time in franchise history gave the Rays three pitchers with double-digit victory totals. By season's end all five starters reached double-digits in wins ... but along with Garza, which of the following made history for the Rays by becoming the first three to hit double-digits in wins during the same season?

- a)   James Shields and Andy Sonnanstine
- b)   James Shields and Edwin Jackson
- c)   Edwin Jackson and Scott Kazmir
- d)   Scott Kazmir and Andy Sonnanstine

QUESTION 97: August 6, 2008, was one of the most important games of the season as the Rays fought to make the playoffs for the first time in franchise history. Facing the dismal Indians at home, the Rays began play with a three-game lead over the Red Sox in the A.L. East but were set to embark on a ten-game road trip immediately following the game. With Scott Kazmir on the mound the Rays jumped out to an early 3-1 lead, but Jhonny Peralta had quite a day for the Tribe, going 5 for 5 with a pair of doubles and a home run, and by the time the ninth inning rolled around the Rays were trailing 7-4. And then the Rays did the unthinkable ... they rallied for six runs without making a single out to win in walk-off fashion, 10-7, something so rare that it was only the third time in the past five decades that a team managed to pull off this extraordinary feat. It ended with a three-run home run by Carlos Peña, which put the club in the right frame of mind heading into the ten-game road trip that many believed would make or break the Rays' season ... but which of the following players delivered a two-run home run that tied the game at 7-7 and set the stage for Peña's game-ending heroics?

- a)   Ben Zobrist
- b)   Carl Crawford

c) Gabe Gross
d) Evan Longoria

QUESTION 98: To follow-up on that last question ... the 2008 Rays were known for late-inning heroics, and believe it or not, Peña's game-winning home run on August 6 was his second game-winning walk-off RBI in a span of four games. On August 3, the Rays scored three runs in the eighth inning vs. Detroit to rally from a 3-1 deficit to take a 4-3 lead ... only to blow that lead in the ninth. In the tenth, the Tigers took a 5-4 lead and sent closer Fernando Rodney to the mound to try and put away the Rays. Yeah, good luck with that. A walk to Willy Aybar got the inning started. Shawn Riggans got hit by a pitch to put two on and no out. Akinori Iwamura bunted the runners over to second and third and up stepped B.J. Upton, who promptly walked to load the bases for Carl Crawford, who delivered a base hit to left field that tied the game and left the bases loaded for Evan Longoria with one out. And Longo ... well, he's occasionally human after all, and he struck out. But the way the 2008 Rays' offense worked, man it was tough, you got Longo you still had to get Los, you know? And that didn't happen. Peña delivered the win in walk-off fashion ... but how?

a) Home run
b) Single
c) Walk
d) Hit by pitch

QUESTION 99: Joe Maddon spent 31 seasons working in the Angels organization, including six as bench coach for Mike Scioscia, before taking over managerial duties for the Rays. His new team promptly lost the first eight games Maddon managed in his return trips to Anaheim ... but when the Rays finally got Maddon a win in his old stomping grounds, they did it in a big way and with a franchise first.

Tampa beat Anaheim 13-4 on June 9, 2008, paced by back-to-back-to-back home runs in the second inning. It was the first time in franchise history that the Rays hit three consecutive homers. Which three hitters are in the record book for this franchise first?

    a)   Ben Zobrist, Evan Longoria, Carlos Peña
    b)   Evan Longoria, Willy Aybar, Dioner Navarro
    c)   Carlos Peña, Willy Aybar, Gabe Gross
    d)   Jason Bartlett, B.J. Upton, Carl Crawford

QUESTION 100: Not every Rays' first-round draft pick has panned out … but for the most part the organization has done a great job drafting and developing its own talent. Which of the following first-round draft picks by the Rays was the 2002 Baseball America Minor League Player of the Year?

    a)   Carl Crawford
    b)   Rocco Baldelli
    c)   Josh Hamilton
    d)   Scott Kazmir

BOTTOM OF THE FIFTH ANSWER KEY

___ QUESTION 91: C*
___ QUESTION 92: B*
___ QUESTION 93: C
___ QUESTION 94: C
___ QUESTION 95: C
___ QUESTION 96: A
___ QUESTION 97: C*
___ QUESTION 98: C*
___ QUESTION 99: B
___ QUESTION 100: B

KEEP A RUNNING TALLY OF YOUR CORRECT ANSWERS!

Number correct: ___ / 10

Overall correct: ___ / 100

#91 – Peña's extra-inning home run was his fourth since 2008. His four homers and ten RBIs in extra-innings during that span were the highest totals of any MLB player.

#92 – Crawford hit a three-run walk-off homer vs. Boston with two outs in the ninth to give the Rays a 6-4 victory on Opening Day 2003 ... but Tampa then lost four straight and five of six.

#97 – Gross was 0 for 3 with a strikeout before hitting one off the back wall to tie the game—it was a *bomb*. And ... the Rays went 7-3 on the road trip and returned home having *increased* their lead over Boston to 4.5 games. One final note ... Peña's homer made him just the tenth player in MLB history to hit a walk-off home run for four different teams: Oakland, Detroit, Boston, and of course, Tampa.

#98 – Okay, so you think a "walk" walk-off win is lame, but let me tell you ... I was there for the walk version and I was there for the three-run bomb that nearly put a hole in the restaurant in centerfield ... *loved them both the same folks, it's about winning.*

Carl Crawford – courtesy author.

Sixth

THE PERFECT STORM ... it is perhaps the most appropriate nickname for any current player in professional baseball. Joe Maddon offered this assessment: "He's such a unique player in today's game. He's so strong, one of the strongest runners I've seen. He covers an incredible amount of turf in the outfield. He's a slasher, can really put the ball in the gaps. If you make a mistake, he can go really deep to right-center."

That sums it up quite well ...

The Perfect Storm—Carl Crawford.

He's been the face of the franchise for the better part of a decade—but make no mistake, Crawford would have been the face of any franchise during that time, he's that good. In high school he was a three-sport star: baseball, basketball, and football. The Houston native was offered a scholarship to run the option for the University of Nebraska football team ... and he was offered a scholarship to be the point guard for the UCLA basketball team. The Rays also made him a second-round draft pick in 1999— and the only reason he was still available that *late* in the draft was the scholarship offers already hanging in the balance.

He chose the Rays—and the rest, as they say, is history ... literally. Crawford begins the second phase of his career in 2011 with the Boston Red Sox, but he leaves as the Rays' franchise leader in career average, RBIs, hits, doubles, triples, extra-base hits, runs, stolen bases, times on base, total bases, sacrifice flies, and games played.

He's only third though in career home runs ...

We can let that one slide though, because his career numbers came with some great memories: two walk-off hits on Opening Day, six steals in a game vs. Boston, a straight steal of home vs. Boston, four All-Star appearances, bringing that home run back in the

2009 All-Star Game to earn MVP honors, four stolen bases titles, a Silver Slugger and a Gold Glove in the same season, 105 triples, and every one of them a great memory for those lucky enough to see one in person, and 215 doubles, all of which we were cheering him to try for three ...

And in his final season with the Rays, Crawford became just the eighth player in baseball's modern era to reach these career milestones: 100 home runs, 100 triples, and 400 stolen bases. He also reached those milestones faster than anyone else in history ... well, Crawford *is* fast, after all—we all know that—but the pace at which he reached those milestones was ridiculous, even for him: he was 29 years, 24 days old. To gain perspective, the previous age of the fastest person to reach those milestones belonged to Hall of Famer Lou Brock: 32 years, 11 months, 11 days.

Crawford beat him by almost four years.

Man, that's not even a race.

Back to the questions ... some tough franchise firsts here in the Sixth, but in the bottom of the frame there's a few softballs to get you back in the game.

TOP OF THE SIXTH

QUESTION 101: He threw the first pitch in franchise history on March 31, 1998, vs. Detroit. It was a ball to Brian Hunter. A lefty, he struggled to a 6-14 record in the team's inaugural season. He wore #40. Who is he?

QUESTION 102: This player was born in Tampa, but played in Toronto, San Diego, and Atlanta before suiting up for Tampa's inaugural game. He wore #29. Who is he?

QUESTION 103: He got the first hit in franchise history, a single against Detroit's Justin Thompson in the bottom of the third inning. He was a lefty outfielder who wore #14, and after his playing career he became a Rays' coach. Who is he?

QUESTION 104: He got the first extra-base hit in franchise history, a double against Justin Thompson in the bottom of the fifth inning. Originally drafted by Boston, he made his big league debut in 1992 with the Red Sox—but in 1998 he was the first catcher in Rays' history, and he spent five seasons sharing time behind the dish at The Trop. His primary jersey was #23, but he initially wore #6 for Tampa. Who is he?

QUESTION 105: He hit the first home run in franchise history, a two-run blast against Justin Thompson in the bottom of the sixth inning (Tampa trailed 11-0 at the time)—and the club later retired his #12 jersey. Who is he?

QUESTION 106: On April 1, 1998, he earned the first win in franchise history, 11-8 vs. Detroit. He pitched six innings and gave up four earned runs. He led the pitching staff with a 14-12 record that season, thus becoming the first name in the franchise record book for most wins in a season. What's remarkable is that he was a 29-year-old rookie! He also became the first All-Star in franchise history and wore #30. Who is he?

QUESTION 107: Tampa's bullpen didn't record its first save that inaugural season until April 12—the tenth game of the season. It wasn't because the team hadn't won any games, either. After beating the Chicago White Sox 4-1 on April 12, the club improved to 6-4 on the season. On April 19, Tampa moved to four games over .500 after taking three games in a four-game series vs. Anaheim—but that was the high water mark during Tampa's first season of play. As for that first save ... it was the first of 26 on the season for this hard-throwing righty who wore #39. Who is he?

QUESTION **108:** Is it possible for *two* players to get credit for being the *first* in franchise history to accomplish something? Actually, yes ... at least when the first stolen base in franchise history is also a double-steal. It happened on April 1, 1998, in the second game of the season. Tampa led Detroit 6-4 in the bottom of the sixth when these two players pulled off a double-steal of second and third—thus becoming the first players in franchise history to steal a base and the first to pull off a double-steal. Lead off man and centerfielder Quinton McCracken, who wore #3, stole third. Batting second, playing second, and stealing second was this player, who wore #13—who is he?

QUESTION **109:** The first cycle in franchise history wasn't until October 2, 2009, vs. CC Sabathia and the New York Yankees. This Rays' player was 5 for 5 with a triple in the first and a double in the third against Sabathia, who was long gone by the time this player homered in the fourth. This outfielder, who wore #2, batted again in the fifth with the Rays up 11-1 ... and he singled to complete the cycle. Who is he?

QUESTION **110:** It took Tampa 29 games to hit a grand slam. The first in franchise history came on May 3, 1998, vs. Charles Nagy and the Cleveland Indians. The guy who hit it was also the first DH in franchise history and he wore #44. It was his third of 17 home runs on the season—a total that was second on the club behind Fred McGriff. Who is he?

TOP OF THE SIXTH ANSWER KEY

___ **QUESTION 101:** Wilson Álvarez
___ **QUESTION 102:** Fred McGriff
___ **QUESTION 103:** Dave Martinez
___ **QUESTION 104:** John Flaherty
___ **QUESTION 105:** Wade Boggs
___ **QUESTION 106:** Rolando Arrojo*
___ **QUESTION 107:** Roberto Hernández
___ **QUESTION 108:** Miguel Cairo
___ **QUESTION 109:** B.J. Upton*
___ **QUESTION 110:** Paul Sorrento

KEEP A RUNNING TALLY OF YOUR CORRECT ANSWERS!

Number correct: ___ / 10

Overall correct: ___ / 110

#106 – He also pitched the first complete game shutout in franchise history, vs. Minnesota on April 30, 1998.

#109 – What makes a cycle even more impressive? Upton also stole home in the same game. It was the first time in nearly a decade that a player hit for the cycle and stole home in the same game.

BOTTOM OF THE SIXTH

QUESTION 111: There have been 13 expansion teams during Major League Baseball's expansion era. Of those, 11 had a pitcher reach 100 career starts within five seasons of beginning play. It took the Colorado Rockies eight years—and it took the Rays the longest. Who was the first pitcher in Rays' franchise history to make 100 career starts—James Shields or Scott Kazmir?

QUESTION 112: To follow-up on that last question— which Rays' pitcher is the franchise leader for career starts—James Shields or Scott Kazmir?

QUESTION 113: And staying with James Shields and Scott Kazmir for one more question ... which one of them has started more Opening Day games than any other pitcher in franchise history?

QUESTION 114: Until 2008, when Tampa suddenly became relevant in terms of playoff contenders, the Rays' best players often toiled in obscurity. Here's a perfect example—in 2005, this reliever was eighth in the majors with 41 saves, but the Rays won only 67 games all season! He was the only pitcher in baseball that season to save 40-plus games for a team with a losing record, and historically he was just the fourth closer to save 40-plus games for a 90-loss team ... and, only five other closers since saves became an official statistic in 1969 managed to save a greater percentage of their team's wins. Who put up such great numbers in an otherwise dismal season—Danys Báez or Roberto Hernández?

QUESTION 115: Sticking with relievers ... here's one who contributed greatly to the Rays' turnaround in 2008, posting some of the best numbers out of the pen of any reliever in baseball. Among relievers he tied for the team lead in wins, but led in earned run average, opponent's average, and strikeouts per nine innings with 12.65—a number that also led all of baseball. Incredibly, he struck out 36.6 percent of all batters he faced, which was the third highest percentage for a reliever in American League history. Who posted such gaudy numbers in 2008—J.P. Howell or Grant Balfour?

QUESTION 116: And one more with Howell and Balfour as your choices ... also in 2008, one of them became the first reliever in nearly two decades to earn three wins in three consecutive appearances while pitching a minimum of two scoreless innings in all three outings. In fact, he pitched three scoreless innings on May 8 to beat the Blue Jays; he pitched three scoreless innings on May 11 to beat the Angels; and he pitched two scoreless innings on May 13 to beat the Yankees ... that's pretty much the definition of a workhorse. Who was it—J.P. Howell or Grant Balfour?

QUESTION 117: In 2008, Tampa was 78-47 with him in the lineup but only 19-18 when he missed time due to injury. That same season the Tampa Bay Chapter of the BBWAA named him the Rays' Most Valuable Player. Who is this star—Jason Bartlett or Carl Crawford?

QUESTION 118: This pitcher tossed a complete game two-hit shutout vs. the Red Sox on April 27, 2008 ... and then two starts later he tossed a complete game one-hit shutout vs. the Angels. Against the Angels, the game was scoreless until Evan Longoria hit a two-run walk-off bomb in the home half of the ninth. It was only the fourth time in baseball's modern era that a walk-off home run won a game in which the winning pitcher tossed a complete game one-hit shutout. As for the starting pitcher with two impressive shutouts early in 2008, he was the first pitcher since Mike Scott (Houston Astros, 1987) to notch a pair of shutouts while allowing two or fewer hits within his first eight starts of a season.

Who was red hot to start the 2008 season—Edwin Jackson or James Shields?

QUESTION 119: Evan Longoria was such a highly touted prospect that he was the subject of a *Sports Illustrated* feature article *before* he made his MLB debut. After he debuted on April 12, 2008, it took him just three games before he launched his first Major League home run. And living up to all the hype, against which rival did Longo blast his first homer—the Boston Red Sox or the New York Yankees?

QUESTION 120: This player tied a franchise record for rookies when he collected three extra-base hits, including his first big league homer, on September 14, 2009, in an 8-4 victory vs. Baltimore. That same season he was the starting shortstop for the International League at the Class-AAA All-Star Game and he was named the International League's best defensive shortstop for the second consecutive season as well as *Baseball America's* No. 5 prospect in the Rays organization. With Jason Bartlett now with the Padres for 2011, this player is projected to be the Rays' starting shortstop. Who is he—Sean Rodriguez or Reid Brignac?

Bottom of the Sixth Answer Key

___ **Question 111:** Scott Kazmir*
___ **Question 112:** James Shields
___ **Question 113:** James Shields
___ **Question 114:** Danys Báez
___ **Question 115:** Grant Balfour
___ **Question 116:** J.P. Howell
___ **Question 117:** Jason Bartlett
___ **Question 118:** James Shields
___ **Question 119:** New York Yankees
___ **Question 120:** Reid Brignac

Keep a running tally of your correct answers!

Number correct: ___ / 10

Overall correct: ___ / 120

#111 – It took the Rays 11 years. Kazmir beat the Yankees 5-2 on May 15, 2008, in his 100th career start.

Seventh

HONDO JUNIOR COLLEGE—also known as the old stomping grounds for ... *Evan Longoria?* Well, yes, that is correct. A product of St. John Bosco in Bellflower, California, the same high school that produced Nomar Garciaparra, Longo's options after graduation were limited. Undrafted and with little to no interest from any Division I schools, Evan Longoria began his ascent to superstardom by playing JuCo ... but you probably noticed it didn't take long for his stock to increase in value. In fact, Longo's rise to stardom has been meteoric.

His freshman year was spent playing JuCo, but as a sophomore he was at Long Beach State, and as a junior in 2006 he was the Big West Conference co-Player of the Year, a finalist for the Golden Spikes Award as the best amateur player in the country, and the overall number three pick during the first-round of Major League Baseball's June Amateur Draft.

It took him about 20 minutes to sign his first contract and then he was off to Hudson (SS-A) where he hung around for a little more than 20 minutes, but not much. In his first season as a professional it took him only 36 games to reach Class-AA. He made that first stop at Hudson Valley for eight games and another at Visalia (A) for 28 games, but very quickly he was in Montgomery (AA). In all three stops he combined to bat .315 with 18 home runs and 58 RBIs in only 62 games.

By the end of 2007 he'd played 31 games at Class-AAA Durham.

In 2008, he played another seven games for Durham, but then on April 12, just 22 months and five days after being drafted, he was the starting third baseman for the Tampa Bay Rays. Six days later the Rays locked him up long-term, signing him to a six-year deal worth nearly $18 million in guaranteed money—but immediately he donated nearly $1 million towards the Rays Baseball Foundation.

Carl Crawford was still the face of the franchise,

and more than a few heads around The Trop collectively shook in unison at the decision to sign Longoria to such a long-term deal—but in hindsight it was both brilliant and a bargain. The day was quickly coming when Crawford would be a free agent and the Rays would not be able to afford him. It might not have been clear around the league just yet, but it was clear to Rays' management that Longoria was going to be the new face of the franchise. And as quickly as he climbed through the ranks to make it to the big club, he also wasted no time in proving that he belonged.

At the All-Star break he was batting .275 with 16 home runs—and he made the A.L. squad by winning the "Final Man" vote-off against four other players. That made him a big league All-Star just 25 months and three days after signing that first contract—and it's probably worth mentioning that despite being a rookie he was also selected to participate in the annual Home Run Derby, becoming the first player in franchise history to do so.

The best part ... we're still discussing Act I.

Evan Longoria ... 2008 American League Rookie of the Year ... same season, homered on the first pitch he saw in the postseason ... same game, homered in his second-ever postseason at bat ... same postseason, six home runs combined in the Division Series and ALCS, tied for the most in history.

It's hard to dismiss the obvious symmetry between Longo and the franchise for which he's now the poster-child: for the player, Hondo Junior College to MLB All-Star ... for the team, worst to first.

As for Act II, sit back and enjoy ... it ain't over yet.

Now more trivia ... almost stretch time here in the Seventh, but don't relax too much, as you're about to find out the questions are amped up a bit. Hey, late-inning pressure situations are a plenty ... deal with it, *be clutch!*

TOP OF THE SEVENTH

QUESTION 121: Carl Crawford set a new franchise record when he stole 55 bases in 2003 (the current franchise record also belongs to Crawford: 60, in 2009). Prior to 2003, however, the most steals by a Rays' player was 31. Whose record did Crawford break in 2003—Jason Tyner or Randy Winn?

QUESTION 122: This player won team MVP honors in 2005 after batting .286 and leading the club with 28 home runs and a then-franchise record 117 RBIs. He also led the Rays with 69 extra-base hits, 40 doubles, and a .325 average with runners in scoring position. Who was the Rays' MVP in 2005—Jorge Cantú or Aubrey Huff?

QUESTION 123: Quinton McCracken set a franchise record during Tampa's inaugural 1998 season with an 18-game hitting streak. That record stood until 2009, when this player hit safely in 19 consecutive games. Who set this new franchise record—Evan Longoria or Jason Bartlett?

QUESTION 124: In 2005, Jorge Cantú hit safely in 11 consecutive games to start the season. An impressive start, but his streak fell two games short of the franchise record 13-game hitting streak to begin a season that this player established in 2003. Who set this franchise record—Aubrey Huff or Rocco Baldelli?

QUESTION 125: In his Major League debut, this Rays' pitcher tossed seven innings vs. Detroit and gave up just one earned run on three hits—and his nine strikeouts are the most in franchise history for any pitcher making his first big league start. He came out of the game leading 3-1, but unfortunately the bullpen gave up a grand slam in the ninth and he was denied his first big league win. Who earned a spot in the franchise record book during his big league debut—Wade Davis or Jeff Niemann?

QUESTION 126: The Rays didn't draft this prospect until the 34th round ... but when he pitched for the Rays' Fall Instructional League team that same year he did not give up any earned runs in 38 innings of work! Two years later, he pitched the first perfect game in the Rays' organization during his very first start of Class-AA ball. It was only the second perfect game in the 138-year history of the Southern League ... and two weeks later, he made his big league debut as the youngest player in Rays' history at 20 years, four months. Who went from the 34th round of the draft to the majors in such unexpected fashion—Chad Gaudin or Doug Waechter?

QUESTION 127: This player was the Class-A Bakersfield Player of the Year after he became just the second Rays' prospect to hit 30 homers in a minor league season. He lost the California League home run title, however, when a player named Jorge Soto hit his 31st home run in his final at bat of the season—which prevented this player from joining his brother, who won the NY Penn League home run title that same season, as the first brothers to win minor league home run titles in the same season since 1929! Even more remarkable is that despite being only 22 years old, he suffered a heart attack that same offseason. And yet that didn't stop him ... three years later he was third on the Rays in home runs. Who is this resilient slugger—Damon Hollins or Jonny Gomes?

QUESTION 128: This player started six games as quarterback for the Auburn Tigers as a true freshman for Coach Terry Bowden. He passed for 1,222 yards and seven touchdowns, but left the program to concentrate on his baseball career (his father had also played at Auburn and later in the NFL). In 2008, he had three of the Rays remarkable 11 walk-off hits, and 14 of his 38 RBIs either tied the game or gave the Rays the lead. Who is this clutch hitter—Eric Hinske or Gabe Gross?

QUESTION **129:** A lot is made, and rightfully so, of the exclusive 30/30 club. No member of the Rays has finished a season with 30 homers and 30 steals ... but this player was the first in franchise history to hit 20 home runs while stealing at least ten bases. Who did this first—Jose Cruz, Jr. or Gerald Williams?

QUESTION **130:** To follow-up on that last question ... there have been seven players through 2010 who have hit 20 homers with at least ten steals for the Rays. Carl Crawford is not one of them—though he hit 19 home runs in 2010 to set a new career high. Along with Jose Cruz, Jr. and Gerald Williams, Greg Vaughn, B.J. Upton, Eric Hinske, and Ben Zobrist are all on the list ... along with this player, the most recent to achieve this feat. Who had at least 20 homers and at least ten steals in 2010 for the Rays—Evan Longoria or Carlos Peña?

TOP OF THE SEVENTH ANSWER KEY

___ **QUESTION 121:** Jason Tyner
___ **QUESTION 122:** Jorge Cantú
___ **QUESTION 123:** Jason Bartlett
___ **QUESTION 124:** Rocco Baldelli
___ **QUESTION 125:** Wade Davis*
___ **QUESTION 126:** Chad Gaudin
___ **QUESTION 127:** Jonny Gomes*
___ **QUESTION 128:** Gabe Gross
___ **QUESTION 129:** Gerald Williams*
___ **QUESTION 130:** Evan Longoria

KEEP A RUNNING TALLY OF YOUR CORRECT ANSWERS!

Number correct: ___ / 10

Overall correct: ___ / 130

#125 – It was on September 6, 2009. Incidentally, his first cousin is Jody Davis, the former All-Star catcher for the Chicago Cubs.

#127 – His breakout minor league season and his heart attack were in 2002.

#129 – Williams did it in 2000 with 21 homers and 12 steals (he was also thrown out attempting to steal 12 times) but Jose Cruz, Jr. also did this—in 2004 with 21 homers and 11 steals.

BOTTOM OF THE SEVENTH

QUESTION 131: His breakout season was 2008, when this reliever led all of baseball by allowing only 11.8 percent of his inherited runners to score. He also tied for the A.L. lead with 92 strikeouts in relief, and he also tied a franchise record by winning his first six decisions of the season—although he was the first to do so as a reliever. Who is this stalwart reliever?

QUESTION 132: The answer to this question might surprise you ... but during the Rays' Pennant-winning 2008 season, who was the team leader in hits, runs, at bats, and games played? He was also second on the team in triples and total bases.

QUESTION 133: He was the Player of the Year for Durham in 2008 and earned a call-up to the Rays on September 9. After battling flight delays all day, he arrived at Fenway Park in time to hit a game-tying pinch-hit home run against Red Sox ace closer Jonathan Papelbon in the ninth inning—and the Rays went on to win 5-4, which had huge implications in the Rays' push to make the postseason. Who hit this dramatic home run?

QUESTION 134: In 2005, this infielder was second on the club in average, hits, and steals ... despite setting career highs in all three categories: .295, 185 hits, and 39 steals. He actually led all MLB players at his position in average, doubles, triples, RBIs, and steals. He also became just the fifth player in franchise history to surpass 180 hits in a season, and he actually set a franchise record by swiping third base 12 times. Who is this infielder that had a career year in 2005?

QUESTION 135: This Rays' pitcher stands 6' 9" but as a middle school student in Houston he was cut from the basketball team ... probably sounds like an oversight on the part of the coach, but then again, Emeka Okafor was his competition during tryouts (and yes, NBA star Okafor made the team). You might say things worked out anyway—in his first season with the Rays he led all Major League rookies in innings, all A.L. rookies in winning percentage, complete games, and shutouts, and his winning percentage was the fifth highest in history for an A.L. rookie with at least 30 starts. Who is this star pitcher?

QUESTION 136: Victor Zambrano beat Oakland and Boston in fine form during his final two home starts of 2003—he tossed a complete game with eight strikeouts vs. Oakland and he went eight innings with six strikeouts vs. Boston. He then began 2004 by beating New York twice and Baltimore once during his first three starts—all at home—making Zambrano the first pitcher in franchise history to win five consecutive home starts. Although, his first start in 2004 was actually in Japan, at the Tokyo Dome, where the club played New York twice to begin the season—but Tampa was technically the home team, and when the series continued a week later at The Trop, Zambrano actually beat the Yankees and Mike Mussina in both games one and three of a four-game series. Two members of the Rays' pitching staff tied that record in 2009. Andy Sonnanstine won five consecutive home starts in May and June, defeating Boston, Cleveland, Kansas City, Washington, and Philadelphia. And then later in 2009, this rookie also tied this franchise record with one of his wins coming against Roy Halladay. He later beat Halladay a second time in 2009, and he also defeated the Yankees at season's end to prevent CC Sabathia from reaching 20 wins for the first time in his career. Who was the Rays' rookie to win five consecutive home starts in 2009?

QUESTION 137: The Rays acquired him in September 2009 as the "player to be named later" that completed the deal sending Scott Kazmir to the Angels ... and he's slated to be the every day second baseman in 2011. Who is this player?

QUESTION 138: In 2009, this Rays' reliever finished with 69 appearances—just one more and he would've hit 70 appearances for five consecutive seasons. Also in 2009, opponents batted just .199 against him. That was the 12th lowest average among A.L. relievers, the second lowest average on the team, and the second consecutive season he held opponents below .200 ... and righties hit only .156 against him. At one point he strung together 14 consecutive scoreless appearances, and he was even better during interleague play, when he retired 25 of 29 batters he faced. Which Rays' reliever put up such good numbers in 2009?

QUESTION 139: In addition to being an All-Star in 2009, he was selected by the Tampa Bay Chapter of the BBWAA as the team MVP. Also, his wife is a contemporary Christian recording artist. Can you name this All-Star?

QUESTION 140: Talk about an epic match-up ... on September 13, 2010, the Rays hosted the Yankees at The Trop with first place in the A.L. East hanging in the balance. New York led by half a game and sent CC Sabathia and his 19 wins to the mound, Tampa countered with David Price and his 17 wins—and neither disappointed. Sabathia gave up just two hits over eight scoreless innings, while Price gave up just three hits over eight scoreless. In the ninth inning and the outcome resting with the bullpens, Carl Crawford was ejected for arguing balls and strikes. His replacement had played just five games since being recalled from the minors on September 1 ... but in the 11th inning that same replacement blasted a 3-2 pitch from Sergio Mitre into the right field bleachers for a walk-off win. He later called it, "Unbelievable ... you just feel like you're floating on clouds." It not only put the Rays back in first,

Andy Sonnanstine

but it was the first time in franchise history that the Rays won a walk-off by a score of 1-0. Who got this huge hit?

Bottom of the Seventh Answer Key

___ **Question 131:** J.P. Howell
___ **Question 132:** Akinori Iwamura
___ **Question 133:** Dan Johnson*
___ **Question 134:** Julio Lugo
___ **Question 135:** Jeff Niemann
___ **Question 136:** David Price
___ **Question 137:** Sean Rodriguez
___ **Question 138:** Dan Wheeler*
___ **Question 139:** Ben Zobrist
___ **Question 140:** Reid Brignac

Keep a running tally of your correct answers!

Number correct: __ / 10

Overall correct: __ / 140

#133 – Refer back to question #73 if you need to … but you probably recall it was also Johnson who hit his first career walk-off home run on August 28, 2010, also against the Red Sox, also in the midst of a Pennant race. Joe Maddon said later, "In the year 2100, they're going to be talking about Dan Johnson and what he did against the Red Sox in '08 and '10. It's awesome."

#138 – Wheeler is also the son-in-law of Rays' broadcaster Dewayne Staats.

Eighth

THE YOUNG GUNS was a phrase used frequently to describe the Atlanta Braves pitching rotation during the 1990s. Atlanta was a franchise accustomed to losing prior to 1991, but in one magical "worst to first" season the Braves proved the old adage really is true: *good pitching really does stop good hitting.*

In 1990, Atlanta was better than average on offense—but with a 4.58 team earned run average, the Braves' pitching staff was the worst in the league. And the team was a league worst 65-97.

In 1991, Atlanta was again better than average on offense—but with a 3.49 team earned run average that was third best in the league, the Braves were 94-68, good for the second best record in the league and a Division Title. Atlanta went on to win the N.L. Pennant before losing the World Series to the Minnesota Twins—and it's worth noting, the Braves lost that series after the Twins' Jack Morris pitched a *ten-inning 1-0 shutout in Game 7.*

Baseball really is a glorified game of throw and catch.

And if you don't have guys who throw it really well, you can't compete for long. Tom Glavine, Steve Avery, and John Smoltz were the Braves' original Young Guns—and after adding Greg Maddux to the mix, Atlanta's starting pitchers won six Cy Young Awards during the 1990s and the Braves began a run of 14 consecutive Division Titles.

The "worst to first" comparison with the Rays is pretty obvious ... if this were a screenplay we'd title it *The Young Guns II.*

In 2007, the Rays' pitching staff led the league in two categories: strikeouts (good) and home runs allowed (not so good). With a 5.53 team earned run average that was the worst in the league, Tampa won 66 games. The bullpen (with very few opportunities) saved a league-worst 28 games.

In 2008, the Rays' pitching staff gave up fewer home runs (good) but also struck out fewer batters (didn't matter) ... but with a 3.83 team earned run average that was the *second lowest in the league*, Tampa won 97 games, good for the second highest total in the league and a Division Title—and of course, we won the Pennant as well. It's also worth noting, the bullpen (with many more opportunities) saved 52 games, the second highest total in the league.

The Young Guns II, starring James Shields, Andy Sonnanstine, Matt Garza, Edwin Jackson, and Scott Kazmir. Also starring out of the bullpen, Troy Percival, whose *28 saves equaled the team total from the previous season*, J.P. Howell, Dan Wheeler, Grant Balfour, and Trever Miller.

In 2010, the Rays' staff was statistically even better. The starting cast of David Price, Matt Garza, James Shields, Jeff Niemann, and Wade Davis, and the supporting bullpen of Rafael Soriano, Lance Cormier, Joaquin Benoit, Dan Wheeler, Grant Balfour, and Randy Choate combined for a 3.78 earned run average that was second lowest in the league and 51 saves that led the league. The staff also gave up the second lowest hits, runs, and earned runs totals—while posting the second highest strikeouts total. And oh yeah ... 96 wins, best in the league.

All five starters in 2010 won at least 12 games, and the oldest among them was James Shields ... he was 28.

Young Guns, indeed.

Bobby Cox had Leo Mazzone ... Joe Maddon has Jim Hickey.

The Braves had the original Young Guns ... the Rays have the current Young Guns. The Braves' strong arms carried the club to 14 Division Titles. The Rays are at two—and counting—and back for an encore at The Trop in 2011 ...

Now on to the Eighth, only 60 questions left, and no margin for error if you want to score a high IQ ...

TOP OF THE EIGHTH

QUESTION 141: Carl Crawford was the face of the Rays' franchise for the better part of a decade ... now that distinction belongs to Evan Longoria. Which one of these All-Stars signed with the Rays out of high school—Carl Crawford or Evan Longoria?

QUESTION 142: Among his career highlights ... in 2009 this Rays' pitcher was the first to start a game at the new Yankee Stadium and he carried a four-hit shutout into the eighth inning before getting a no-decision. In a game against Cleveland he also batted in the third hole in place of Evan Longoria ... no kidding. Longo was mistakenly listed at 3B instead of DH, forcing this pitcher to bat third. He was 1 for 3 with an RBI double. Who is this pitcher—James Shields or Andy Sonnanstine?

QUESTION 143: Also in the category of career highlights ... in 2008 this Rays' pitcher became the first in franchise history to win four games in April. Who is this pitcher—James Shields or Andy Sonnanstine?

QUESTION 144: In eight seasons before Joe Maddon took over as manager of the Rays, the ballclub finished dead last in the division seven times. The best finish before Maddon took over was a fourth-place showing under this skipper—Lou Piniella or Hal McRae?

QUESTION 145: Which two players were the only members of the Rays to lead the A.L. in a statistically significant offensive category during 2010—Carl Crawford and Ben Zobrist or Evan Longoria and Carlos Peña?

QUESTION 146: When asked who would win the 2008 All-Star Home Run Derby, this Rays' participant replied, "Josh Hamilton will win." Well, he was right about Hamilton, formerly a Rays' top draft pick, putting on the most impressive show in Derby history (28 homers in the first round!)—in the end, however, it was Twins' first baseman Justin Morneau who eventually won. As for this member of the Rays, despite hitting only three home runs and not making it out of the first round, he *was* the first player in franchise history to be invited to participate in the annual Home Run Derby. Who is this player—Carlos Peña or Evan Longoria?

QUESTION 147: This Rays' prospect got his first big league hit on September 11, 2010. It got a bit lost amidst a grand slam from Brad Hawpe and a dominating pitching performance from Wade Davis in a 13-1 rout of the Toronto Blue Jays ... but it's not a moment he'll ever forget. He was 0 for 5 in his first three games before delivering a pinch-hit double in the eighth inning. After the game he said, "It feels good. It took forever. Definitely a special moment." Which prospect got his first big league hit in September 2010—Desmond Jennings or Nevin Ashley?

QUESTION 148: This Rays' reliever said, "I was angry. I was upset. I told myself, 'I'm going to prove them wrong.'" And what was he referring to? Well, it seems he was one of the last players cut from the Opening Day roster in 2008 when he was designated for assignment on March 30. He went to Class-AAA Durham, but ... at the time he made that statement he had just earned his fourth save of the season for the Rays as he filled in for injured closer Troy Percival. Seems he dominated Class-AAA, got the call back to the big club, and proved to be an integral part of the Rays' bullpen down the stretch and into the postseason. Who is this reliever—J.P. Howell or Grant Balfour?

QUESTION 149: Carl Crawford stole his 300th career base during the Rays' historic 2008 season. It was a steal of second vs. Kansas City, his 23rd stolen base of the season—and with it he not only got a standing ovation from the home crowd but he also joined some pretty elite company: only Rickey Henderson, Ty Cobb, Tim Raines, Vince Coleman, César Cedeño, Clyde Milan, Eddie Collins, and Sherry Magee were as young as Crawford when they reached 300 career steals. How old was Carl Crawford when he reached this milestone—26 or 28?

QUESTION 150: And a follow-up now ... Tampa's offense ran all over Boston on May 3, 2009—literally. The Rays set a franchise record by stealing eight bases in the 5-3 victory. Carl Crawford had most of them, tying a Major League record for most steals in a game. How many bases did Crawford steal that day—five or six?

TOP OF THE EIGHTH ANSWER KEY

___ **QUESTION 141:** Carl Crawford
___ **QUESTION 142:** Andy Sonnanstine
___ **QUESTION 143:** Andy Sonnanstine
___ **QUESTION 144:** Lou Piniella
___ **QUESTION 145:** Carl Crawford & Ben Zobrist*
___ **QUESTION 146:** Evan Longoria
___ **QUESTION 147:** Desmond Jennings
___ **QUESTION 148:** Grant Balfour
___ **QUESTION 149:** 26
___ **QUESTION 150:** Six

KEEP A RUNNING TALLY OF YOUR CORRECT ANSWERS!

Number correct: __ / 10

Overall correct: __ / 150

#145 – Crawford in triples, Zobrist in sacrifice flies.

#150 – Crawford also had four hits, making him the first Major League player with four hits and six steals in a game since Hall of Famer Eddie Collins ... in 1912!

BOTTOM OF THE EIGHTH

QUESTION 151: Joe Maddon said of this player: "If you come to the ballpark and you see [him] hit a triple, you've had a pretty good day ... when he hits the ball down the line or in the gap, he's thinking three. Never thinks two. He breaks for a triple. He wants triple, he takes triple." Who is the player Joe Maddon was referring to?

QUESTION 152: He was the third overall pick in the 2006 June Draft, and among college players in that draft he was called the "best pure hitter" by *Baseball America*. Who is this player?

QUESTION 153: In July 2006, Tampa traded one of its best players to the Houston Astros—Aubrey Huff. In return, the Rays got Mitch Talbot and ... this player, who has turned into an All-Star and fan-favorite. Who is he?

QUESTION 154: At one time he was the franchise leader for career home runs ... at present he's second on that list, a spot he'll hold to himself until Evan Longoria bombs another 46 home runs. Hey, it'd be great if Longo caught him in 2011, but it probably won't happen until 2012 ... either way, this player hit 128 home runs for the Rays and yet he claims his career total in high school was ... *one!* Who is this player?

QUESTION 155: The Rays drafted him out of high school as the number two overall pick. Regarded as a five-tool player throughout his minor league career, he ranks among the top ten in franchise history for hits, on-base percentage, slugging percentage, runs, total bases, doubles, triples, home runs, RBIs, and stolen bases ... and his real name is Melvin. By what name is he known as to Rays' fans?

QUESTION 156: Along with Matt Garza, this All-Star came to the Rays in the trade that sent Delmon Young to the Twins. Can you name him?

QUESTION 157: As a 20-year-old he was *Baseball America's* Minor League Player of the Year and as a 21-year-old he was the Rays' starting centerfielder on Opening Day. His first game was against the Boston Red Sox and his first hit was a rocket double against Pedro Martínez. Can you name this long-time fan-favorite?

QUESTION 158: After season totals of 32, 40, 40, 46, and 33 home runs at hitter-friendly Coors Field, he was traded to Tampa where he signed a contract that paid him in excess of $6 million per season. And then he hit a grand total of ... *eight home runs.* That's worth repeating: in 109 games over two seasons—eight home runs. In fairness, he found his swing again after the Rays cut him loose, but who was this slugger that couldn't hit at The Trop?

QUESTION 159: He was the MVP of the 2001 Futures Game and was in the top three in every Triple Crown category in the International League when he was called up to the big club on July 26, 2001—and his five Opening Day starts are the most by a catcher in franchise history. When he left Tampa, it was via trade to the Los Angeles Dodgers ... and in return, the Rays got Dioner Navarro, who made four Opening Day starts as catcher for the Rays—the second most in franchise history. Who is this catcher that made five Opening Day starts for the Rays?

QUESTION 160: After Tampa beat the Chicago White Sox 6-4 on October 2, 2008, in the first postseason game in franchise history, Joe Maddon praised this player by saying: "I wasn't surprised. He's always in the moment. He's always got this way about him that you know ... he's not going to be overwhelmed by the situation. And that speaks beyond his skill level ... in a non-cocky way, he's just very confident." Whose memorable postseason debut was the Rays' manager referring to?

Bottom of the Eighth Answer Key

__ **Question 151:** Carl Crawford
__ **Question 152:** Evan Longoria
__ **Question 153:** Ben Zobrist
__ **Question 154:** Aubrey Huff
__ **Question 155:** B.J. Upton
__ **Question 156:** Jason Bartlett
__ **Question 157:** Rocco Baldelli
__ **Question 158:** Vinny Castilla
__ **Question 159:** Toby Hall
__ **Question 160:** Evan Longoria

Keep a running tally of your correct answers!

Number correct: __ / 10

Overall correct: __ / 160

Ninth

AMERICAN LEAGUE CHAMPIONS ... in a word, extraordinary. That's as close as you can get to describing 2008 in a single word. What the Rays accomplished defied such overwhelming odds in such convincing fashion that 2008 belongs in the same discussion as the comeback made by the Boston Red Sox vs. the New York Yankees during the 2004 American League Championship Series.

Let's examine the case for making such a statement.

The Tampa Bay Devil Rays played 324 games in 1998-99 with obvious, disastrous results—in arguably baseball's toughest Division. The D-Rays never led the Division standings for a single day. The D-Rays never soared higher than four games over .500 at any point in two seasons—and the club finished dead last by a combined 81 games. The club never won more than six games in a row, but lost as many as 11 straight, were shutout 24 times, and lost by five or more runs *64 times.* The club never had a winning record on the road or at home—never even had a winning month until August 1999, and managed to reach .500 in a month only one other time. In two seasons the Devil Rays were a combined 60 games under .500.

But hope springs eternal every spring and, finally, success at last—on April 3, 2000, the Devil Rays shutout the Twins 7-0 on Opening Day ... thus spending one day on top of the Division ... for the season. Never a lead, just tied on top after Opening Day ... but after three years that was the club's biggest success. Another Opening Day win, this time 8-1 vs. Toronto in 2001, and one more day tied at the top ... for a day, after all, the D-Rays proceeded to lose their next seven and finished the month 8-18, dead last, 8.5 games behind the Red Sox. It wasn't until a season-opening sweep vs. Detroit in 2002 that Tampa actually *led* the Division—it was only a half-game lead, and it was only April 4 ... but in its fifth season, Tampa finally spent more than one day on top of the Division, and did it all alone.

And then it was off to New York and a road-sweep at the hands of the hated-Yankees and that, as they say, was that.

All total the Devil Rays were tied or alone in first in the A.L. East for a grand total of 19 days (all in April) in ten seasons from 1998-2007. In that time the club never ventured higher than four games above .500, and in six of those seasons the D-Rays high-water mark was a single game above .500, including three consecutive seasons from 2005-07.

And then came, perhaps, the biggest offseason move in franchise history ... and no, we're not talking about inviting Carlos Peña to camp or hiring Joe Maddon or appointing Andrew Friedman as Executive Vice President of Baseball Operations—those moves had already transpired. No, we're talking about the really big move. After 2007 the Tampa Bay Devil Rays officially released the "Devil" and emerged in 2008 as the Tampa Bay Rays.

That's got to be it, right?

After all, in 2008 Tampa had a winning record in every month except September when it was 13-14. Five consecutive months with a winning record to start the season, after ten previous seasons in which the Rays had never managed more than one winning month in any given season—and three seasons in which the Rays never managed a winning record in a single month.

And the big one: 113 days on top of the Division.

After 19 days in first during ten seasons, 113 days in first in 2008.

After ten seasons of losing in every way imaginable—extra-innings, one-run games, and blowouts—in 2008 the Rays were 10-6 in extra-innings, 29-18 in one-run games, and 27-18 in blowouts (games decided by five or more runs). And don't even get us started on all the walk-off wins ...

After ten seasons in which the Devil Rays had ever won more than 70 games, in 2008 the Rays won *57 games at home* ... after ten seasons in which the Devil Rays had won 30 or more road games only three times, in 2008 the Rays won *40 road games* for the first time in franchise history.

The Rays swept the Boston Red Sox at The Trop from April 25-27, in the first series of the season between the two clubs. Less than a week later, the Rays swept the Red Sox at Fenway from May 2-4. It was the first time in Major League history that the defending World Series champions were swept twice in the same season by a team *defending baseball's worst record.*

Need more to convince you extraordinary is the only word that comes close to describing 2008? Here you go: Tampa swept Boston *a third time*, from June 30 – July 2, to open a 3.5 game lead in the Division ... *and it was the first time since 1997 that a team other than Boston or New York led the A.L. East by that many games, that late in the season*—and it was the first time since *2000 that a team other than Boston or New York led the A.L. East in July or later by any margin, period.*

The first game of the Rays' third sweep of the Red Sox gave Tampa its 50th win of the season ... *that victory made Tampa the first team in Major League history to win 50 games before July 1 after losing 95 or more games in the previous season*—and the final game of the Rays' third sweep of the Red Sox moved Tampa to 20 games above .500 for the first time in franchise history.

Still not convinced?

In the heat of the Pennant race the Rays swept the Red Sox and Blue Jays in consecutive series—it was the first time in franchise history the club swept back-to-back home series of at least three games during the same home stand. Also in a crucial stretch of the season, Andy Sonnanstine polished off a victory vs. St. Louis by giving up just one run in eight innings—that performance capped a ten-game stretch in which Rays' starters surrendered only nine runs ... *in ten games!* How good is that streak? It was only the fifth time in three decades that a group of starters went on a ten-game run that was as impressive as what the Rays did while battling for a postseason berth in 2008.

You need no more proof, we're certain of that—but for good measure, let's close out with some final evidence: *the Rays won 34 series during the regular season, including ten sweeps, eight of which were at home ... the Rays lost only two of their final 23 home series ... the Rays were just the seventh team in four decades to play .700 or better at home ... the Rays won 31 more games than in 2007, which was the third highest turnaround in Major League history ... and it took only 117 games to eclipse the previous franchise record of 70 wins ...*

American League Champions.

In a word ... *extraordinary.*

To the trivia again as we head to the Ninth—use that closer's mentality!

TOP OF THE NINTH

QUESTION 161: This slugger began a very impressive run in 2007 when he was fourth in the league in RBIs and earned Comeback Player of the Year honors and a Silver Slugger Award. He followed that up with a Gold Glove in 2008 and an All-Star appearance in 2009, when he also led the league in home runs and hit the century mark in RBIs for the third consecutive season. Who is this slugger?

QUESTION 162: In the 2010 Division Series vs. Texas the Rays faced a must-win situation on the road in Game 4. And with the season hanging in the balance, Manager Joe Maddon started a rookie catcher *and* a rookie pitcher ... and won. It was the first time since the 1947 World Series that a team started rookie battery mates in the postseason and still won the game. In 1947, it was Spec Shea and Yogi Berra for the Yankees. Can you name the rookie battery mates that beat Texas in Game 4 of the 2010 Division Series for the Rays?

QUESTION 163: Also from the 2010 Division Series vs. Texas ... after losing Games 1 and 2 at home, Tampa was in dire need of someone to step up his game, big time. And this player did exactly that, accomplishing something that no one in MLB postseason history had ever done. In his final two at bats in Game 3 he hit a home run and a single to help Tampa rally for a 6-3 victory. In his first two at bats in Game 4 he hit a triple and an RBI double to help Tampa take the early lead and eventually force a deciding Game 5. That made him the first player to hit a single, double, triple, and a home run in four consecutive postseason at bats. Not bad, right? Who is this clutch performer?

QUESTION 164: In 1987, Eric Davis had 68 RBIs and 33 stolen bases for the Cincinnati Reds ... *before* the All-Star break. It took 23 seasons before another Major League player made it to the break with at least 50 RBIs and 30 steals ... and he did it in 2010 with the Tampa Bay Rays. Who is this player?

QUESTION 165: One member of the Rays hit 20 home runs vs. the Yankees from 2007-10. That's easily the highest total for any one player—on any team—against the Yankees during that span. Who is this slugger the Yankees would prefer to avoid?

QUESTION 166: Tampa traded Bobby Abreu to the Philadelphia Phillies to get this switch-hitting shortstop, who batted .208 during the Rays' inaugural 1998 season. Hey, not all trades work out ... nonetheless, he was the Opening Day shortstop in the first game in franchise history. Can you name him?

QUESTION 167: Here's a move that did work out ... this All-Star signed a football scholarship to play quarterback for the University of Nebraska. He also averaged 27 points a game playing basketball in high school. But ... when drafted by the Rays he chose baseball over football and basketball. Good move—who is this superstar?

QUESTION 168: This Rays' superstar was put on the cover of the video game Major League Baseball 2K10—he also appeared in a commercial for the game, advertising a $1 million prize to the first person to pitch a perfect game. And ironically, that same year he broke up a no-hit bid by Toronto's Brandon Morrow with two outs in the ninth inning ... who is this player?

QUESTION 169: When Carlos Peña hit the century mark in RBIs in 2008 he was just the third player in franchise history to do so in consecutive seasons. The first time a Rays' player performed this feat was from 1999-2000. The second time was from 2003-04. Can you name the two sluggers prior to Peña who reached this milestone in back-to-back campaigns?

QUESTION 170: A lot of professional baseball players were two-sport stars in college or high school, but very few play more than one sport at the professional level. This Rays' pitcher, however, spent four years in the NBA before he decided to give professional baseball a shot—and he led the Rays in wins in back-to-back seasons in 2004-05. And yes, at the time he was the tallest player in franchise history. Can you name him?

TOP OF THE NINTH ANSWER KEY

___ **QUESTION 161:** Carlos Peña
___ **QUESTION 162:** Wade Davis & John Jaso
___ **QUESTION 163:** Carlos Peña
___ **QUESTION 164:** Carl Crawford
___ **QUESTION 165:** Carlos Peña
___ **QUESTION 166:** Kevin Stocker
___ **QUESTION 167:** Carl Crawford
___ **QUESTION 168:** Evan Longoria
___ **QUESTION 169:** Fred McGriff & Aubrey Huff
___ **QUESTION 170:** Mark Hendrickson

KEEP A RUNNING TALLY OF YOUR CORRECT ANSWERS!

Number correct: ___ / 10

Overall correct: ___ / 170

BOTTOM OF THE NINTH

QUESTION 171: The Rays turned the second triple play in franchise history on September 2, 2006. J.P. Howell was on the mound when it happened and he described it this way: "It was the first one I've ever seen, so I'll take that. My theory was just throw a strike and move ... I was wrapped in that so bad, I just watched the ball fly around like a snowball fight. But it was fun, man." Not a bad description of the events, either—because of the more than 500 triple plays turned since 1900 this was the first in Major League history that went like this: 2-6-2. A strikeout and two runners caught stealing—Seattle's Raúl Ibañez struck out swinging with Adrián Béltre running from first on the pitch. The Rays' catcher threw to second, where the shortstop who was covering tagged out Béltre and then fired back to the catcher to cut down José López running from third, trying to steal home. Two Rays' players, one play unique in all of MLB history— who were the catcher and shortstop that turned this historic triple play for the Rays?

QUESTION 172: In Game 1 of the 2008 Division Series vs. the White Sox, one key member of the Rays had to leave the game after two innings because of a scratched cornea that caused blurred vision in his left eye. Which Rays' star was out of action for part of the Division Series due to this freak injury?

QUESTION 173: Also in Game 1 of the 2008 Division Series vs. the White Sox ... Chicago's shortstop and leadoff man Orlando Cabrera had some words with this Rays' reliever during a key moment of the ballgame. Cabrera batted with the bases loaded and two outs in the seventh, and his White Sox were trailing the Rays, 6-3. After the first pitch to him missed outside, Cabrera kicked the dirt around home plate and yelled out something to the effect of "throw it over the plate." This Rays' reliever responded by striking out Cabrera, ending the threat, and then yelling after him, "Go sit down!" After the game he laughed, "I think I might have mixed one or two words in with it." Who is this vocal reliever that got the job done for the Rays in Game 1 of the 2008 Division Series?

QUESTION 174: Rays' pitching coach Jim Hickey said of this player after Game 2 of the 2008 Division Series, "I would say it was an extremely gutsy performance. It was gigantic. The easiest thing in the world would've been to just kind of fold the tent in the first inning." Who was this pitcher that got off to a shaky start, yielding two first inning runs, but then settled in to get the 6-2 win and stake the Rays to a 2-0 series lead vs. the White Sox?

QUESTION 175: After dropping the first game of the 2008 American League Championship Series to the Red Sox, Game 2 of the series proved to be a must-win for the Rays—and it was an epic battle, literally, lasting five hours and 27 minutes and requiring 433 pitches before the Rays won it as they won so many throughout the season: in walk-off fashion. As for the player who tagged and scored the winning run on B.J. Upton's sacrifice fly, Joe Maddon said this: "In a straight up race, I've got him over Seabiscuit." We mentioned this player once already … but can you remember the name of the pinch-runner whose mad dash to the plate gave the Rays a Game 2 victory vs. Boston?

QUESTION 176: In Game 3 of the 2008 American League Championship Series vs. Boston, the Rays faced a starting pitcher who had already beaten Tampa three times during the regular season. With the series tied 1-1 and the scene now shifted to Fenway, it was imperative the Rays find a way to solve this hurler. No problem— just give the ball to Matt Garza and smack four home runs. And that's exactly what the Rays did. Who did the Rays pound 9-1 during Game 3 of the ALCS after losing to him three times during the regular season?

QUESTION 177: After the Rays' 9-1 victory in Game 3, Joe Maddon was asked about one of his players that went yard: "I was very happy for him. Happy for us, but happy for him, too, based on what he's gone through to get to this particular moment, being from this region." Which slugger was Maddon referring to?

QUESTION 178: After this pitcher defeated Tim Wakefield and the Red Sox 13-4 to stake the Rays to a 3-1 lead in the 2008 American League Championship Series—just one win away from the World Series—his parents decided to pay a visit to the Hall of Fame in Cooperstown. You see, on their previous visit to the Hall of Fame they realized their son's file in the A. Bartlett Giamatti Research Center was empty ... but with Game 4 wins in both the Division Series and League Championship Series, along with some key moments during the Rays' historic 2008 season, this player's mother made sure his file wouldn't be empty any longer. She said, "I have been putting together some scrapbooks and I had a box of clippings set aside for the Hall of Fame. It is a little crazy and not in any order, but I will do better next time!" Whose gutsy performances during both Game 4 of the Division Series and Game 4 of the ALCS were definitely worthy of clippings going to the Hall of Fame?

QUESTION 179: After closing out Game 7 of the 2008 ALCS vs. Boston, this pitcher said, "I thought pitching to Pedro Martinez [in a minor league rehab start] was going to be the highlight of my year ... but this? It was unreal." Who made these remarks after getting the save and punching the Rays' ticket to the World Series?

QUESTION 180: In that same Game 7 ... the Rays fell behind when Dustin Pedroia homered as the second batter of the game. After tying the score with a run in the fourth and taking the lead with a run in the fifth, who hit a seventh inning home run that sealed the Rays' 3-1 margin of victory in arguably the most important win in franchise history?

Bottom of the Ninth Answer Key

___ **Question 171:** Dioner Navarro & Ben Zobrist
___ **Question 172:** Carlos Peña
___ **Question 173:** Grant Balfour
___ **Question 174:** Scott Kazmir
___ **Question 175:** Fernando Perez
___ **Question 176:** Jon Lester
___ **Question 177:** Rocco Baldelli
___ **Question 178:** Andy Sonnanstine
___ **Question 179:** David Price
___ **Question 180:** Willy Aybar

Keep a running tally of your correct answers!

Number correct: ___ / 10

Overall correct: ___ / 180

Free Baseball!

THE LONGEST OFFSEASON ... it began October 12, 2010, with nearly 42,000 disappointed fans filing out of Tropicana Field just before midnight. A tough loss, 5-1, to Cliff Lee and the Texas Rangers during Game 5 of the Division Series brought the Rays' postseason run to a premature end.

It was a completely different feeling than 2008, when no one expected a World Series showdown between the Tampa Bay Rays and the Philadelphia Phillies. In 2010, that was exactly the World Series matchup that most people *were* expecting.

Despite that loss, Rays' fans proudly looked back on a three-year run that was the most successful in franchise history and had catapulted the Rays to elite status among Major League teams. But with that loss, Rays' fans also began a long, anxious offseason ... because everyone knew the challenges facing the club, the ones we'd been dreading all throughout the season, were now upon us, and would soon have to be dealt with.

Small market team, big name free agents ... it can be discouraging at times. Okay, most of the time. Well, truthfully, nearly all of the time ... definitely all of the time.

There's nothing wrong with taking stock of what we've lost this offseason. Here's a painful glimpse: Carlos Peña, Carl Crawford, Matt Garza, Jason Bartlett, Dan Wheeler, Grant Balfour, Rafael Soriano, Joaquin Benoit, Lance Cormier, Randy Choate, Rocco Baldelli ... some signed with other clubs, some were traded or retired, you get the picture. That's not the entire list, but it's enough. Word of advice though: let's not waste time lamenting other teams stockpiling big names with large amounts of cash to satisfy a fan-base accustomed to filling its needs through instant gratification. Instead, let's focus on another thought: Don Mattingly.

That's right ... Donnie Baseball. One of the greatest players of his generation, he gave his entire career to the New York Yankees—13 full seasons from 1983-95.

In 110 seasons of play, the Yankees' franchise has been to the postseason 49 times. Or put another way, anyone who has spent 13 seasons wearing pinstripes could reasonably have expected to see postseason action a minimum of five times, closer to six. Don Mattingly made exactly one trip to the postseason—it was 1995, his final season.

The Atlanta Braves, who four years earlier went from "worst to first" to claim the N.L. Pennant, won the 1995 World Series—despite undergoing many, many personnel changes from 1991-95. The reason for the Braves' continued success was consistency from management and the front office that had built a franchise ... not a one-year team.

Don Mattingly got only one chance at the postseason during his playing days because early in his career the Yankees weren't building from within—not nearly enough. It was only as Mattingly was on his way out that the Yankees' farm system meshed with some key signings to produce a playoff-caliber team. And unfortunately for Mattingly, who truly was an extraordinary player and was very deserving of a championship, it was the year after he retired that the Yankees again developed into a dynasty. And as you think about the Yankees' dynasty of the late 1990s, remember guys like Derek Jeter, Bernie Williams, and Mariano Rivera were the key pieces and they all came from within the organization.

Is it possible to buy a championship?

Of course it is.

However, the Braves' Chipper Jones began his career with 11 consecutive trips to the postseason. So far as guys go, he was no more deserving than Don Mattingly. Its true Mattingly didn't play in the Wild Card era until his final season, and it was the Wild Card that let him taste the postseason for the only time ... but *none* of Chipper's 11 consecutive trips to the playoffs were via the Wild Card. So here's the point: Atlanta won the 1995 World Series because a franchise was built around a philosophy that its homegrown talent was taught, believed, lived, and played.

Did big name free agent signings help the Yankees keep winning after the 1990s?

Of course, but do you think Don Mattingly would have preferred playing his career under the philosophy of Joe Maddon and Andrew Friedman or under the philosophy that let him play exactly five games in the playoffs despite playing 13 seasons in the Bronx?

The days and weeks that passed from October 12, 2010, until February 15, 2011, when pitchers and catchers looking to make the Rays' 2011 roster reported to camp, were long and at times painful. We've lost some key guys, but we've also gained some ... but perhaps the most important thing we have, the one thing that hasn't changed for three years now, is a philosophy that also can be taught, believed, lived, and played.

No idea what's in store for the Rays in 2011 and beyond—definitely the past three years have been extraordinary and a high standard has been set. We do know this, however: Joe Maddon believes attitude is a decision. He teaches that philosophy ... *and here's hoping Rays' fans and players alike believe, live, and play it.*

And now we've reached the final questions ... only 20 remain. Be confident, and finish strong!

TOP OF THE TENTH

QUESTION 181: Talk about a storybook season ... who set franchise records for both home runs and RBIs in the same season after he won a starting job as a non-roster invitee to Spring Training?

QUESTION 182: To follow-up on that last question, the previous franchise record for home runs was 34, but the new record *shattered* that number. How many homers did he hit to establish a new franchise record?

QUESTION 183: One more follow-up ... the previous home run record was tied by Aubrey Huff when he hit 34 homers in 2003. In 1999, who became the first player in franchise history to hit 34 home runs in a season?

QUESTION 184: This pitcher earned two road victories in impressive fashion during one week in September 2007. First he tossed seven shutout innings at Fenway Park, striking out ten batters in a 1-0 victory, and then he threw six innings without allowing an earned run vs. Seattle in a 6-2 victory. In 13 innings of work he recorded 21 strikeouts. His strong performances earned him Player of the Week honors for the second time in his career—plus, he became the first pitcher in franchise history to reach 35 career wins. Who is this pitcher?

QUESTION 185: He set a new single-game franchise record when he scored five runs vs. Toronto on May 24, 2006. Who is this speedster?

QUESTION 186: He set a new single-game franchise record when he pounded four doubles vs. the New York Yankees on July 29, 2006, at Yankee Stadium. Remarkably, he hit only 12 doubles all season ... can you name this versatile player (he played 1B, 2B, 3B, SS, and all three outfield positions for the Rays)?

QUESTION 187: This player set or tied four home run related franchise records in 2009. They are: four multi-homer games, three pinch-hit home runs, two grand slams, and 27 home runs by a switch-hitter. Who is this All-Star?

QUESTION 188: Rickey Henderson banged out 47 hits while stealing 22 bases in June 1985. Yes, you read that right—in one month: 47 hits, 22 steals. He was with the Yankees at the time. No one in baseball managed 40 hits and 20 steals in a single month until May 2009, when this member of the Rays did the trick: 43 hits, 21 steals. Who put up these spectacular numbers for the Rays?

QUESTION 189: Here's a rather unique club that at the moment consists of just four members: Odalis Perez, Francisco Rodriguez, Josh Kinney, and ... this Rays' pitcher, who all earned a win pitching in the postseason before earning a Major League win pitching in the regular season. Which Rays' pitcher belongs to this club?

QUESTION 190: Here's another club with limited membership ... in the past 40 years only three times has a rookie hit a grand slam against a pitcher who had previously been selected to at least five All-Star Games. In that third instance, which Rays' rookie hit his first Major League grand slam against Roy Halladay, who at the time was a five-time All-Star?

Top of the Tenth Answer Key

___ **Question 181:** Carlos Peña
___ **Question 182:** 46
___ **Question 183:** Jose Canseco*
___ **Question 184:** Scott Kazmir
___ **Question 185:** Carl Crawford
___ **Question 186:** Tomás Pérez
___ **Question 187:** Ben Zobrist
___ **Question 188:** Carl Crawford
___ **Question 189:** David Price
___ **Question 190:** Evan Longoria

Keep a Running Tally of Your Correct Answers!

Number correct: ___ / 10

Overall correct: ___ / 190

#183 – Canseco took only 81 games to become the first player in franchise history to reach 30 homers when he connected on July 4, 1999. Canseco had 31 homers at the break, but he played only 31 games the second half of the season and finished with 34. That same season, Fred McGriff became the second player in franchise history to reach 30 homers when he connected on September 19. The Crime Dog finished the season with 32 bombs.

BOTTOM OF THE TENTH

QUESTION 191: This player tied a franchise record on July 26, 2008, when he hit two triples in the same game. It wasn't the first time he'd tied that record, either ... or the second, or even the third. It was, astoundingly, the seventh time in his career that he'd hit two triples in the same game—which, obviously, added to yet another franchise record that he already owned. Who is this speedster—Carl Crawford or B.J. Upton?

QUESTION 192: If you hit a home run it feels pretty darn good. If you hit two in a game, well, even better. But if you hit three bombs in one game, well now, that's *spectacular*. Who was the first player in franchise history to blast three homers in one game—Evan Longoria or Jonny Gomes?

QUESTION 193: The franchise single-game record for RBIs is seven. Who is the slugger that set this standard—Fred McGriff or Carlos Peña?

QUESTION 194: This pitcher established a new single-game franchise record with 13 strikeouts vs. Oakland on August 25, 2007. Who is he—Scott Kazmir or James Shields?

QUESTION 195: This pitcher established a new single-game franchise record with seven consecutive strikeouts vs. Florida on June 10, 2007. Who is he—James Shields or Andy Sonnanstine?

QUESTION 196: Delmon Young tied a franchise record in 2007 when he played in all 162 regular season games. Young was just the second player in franchise history to appear in all 162 games during a season. Who was the first—Aubrey Huff or Carl Crawford?

QUESTION 197: The franchise record for most home runs at Tropicana Field during a season is 23. Who set this record—Jose Canseco or Carlos Peña?

QUESTION 198: This slugger set a franchise single-season record for home runs against one team when he blasted eight bombs vs. the New York Yankees in 2007. Who is this slugger—Jonny Gomes or Carlos Peña?

QUESTION 199: This player set a franchise single-season record when he homered to lead off a game five times in 2006. Who is this fan-favorite—Rocco Baldelli or Carl Crawford?

QUESTION 200: This slugger set three franchise single-season records when he pounded out 84 extra-base hits, including 47 doubles, for 353 total bases. Who is he—Evan Longoria or Aubrey Huff?

Bottom of the Tenth Answer Key

__ **Question 191:** Carl Crawford
__ **Question 192:** Jonny Gomes*
__ **Question 193:** Carlos Peña*
__ **Question 194:** Scott Kazmir
__ **Question 195:** Andy Sonnanstine
__ **Question 196:** Aubrey Huff
__ **Question 197:** Carlos Peña*
__ **Question 198:** Carlos Peña
__ **Question 199:** Rocco Baldelli
__ **Question 200:** Aubrey Huff*

Keep a running tally of your correct answers!

Number correct: __ / 10

Overall correct: __ / 200

#192 – Gomes did it on July 30, 2005; Longoria became the second player with a three-homer game when he lit up the Twins on September 18, 2008. Gomes and Longoria also share the franchise record with 12 total bases in a game.

#193 – Peña did it vs. Baltimore on September 5, 2007. He was 2 for 3 with two homers, two walks, four runs, and seven RBIs as Tampa rolled, 17-2. Thanks to Peña, the Rays also established a team single-game record with 41 total bases—a feat matched by the 2009 squad vs. Colorado on June 16.

#197 – Peña hit half of his 46 homers at home and half on the road, which gives him the franchise record for home and road home runs in a season with the exact same number.

#200 – Huff set these records in 2003.

Andy Sonnanstine

Tampa Bay Rays IQ

It's time to find out your Rays IQ. Add your total from all ten chapters and see how you did! Here's how it breaks down:

GENIUS RAYS IQ EXCEEDS CARL CRAWFORD & JOE MADDON	= 190-200
GENIUS RAYS IQ DESTINED TO BE A FIRST BALLOT HALL OF FAMER	= 180-189
GENIUS RAYS IQ IS WORTHY OF A WORLD CHAMPIONSHIP	= 170-179
SUPERIOR RAYS IQ IS WORTHY OF LEGENDARY STATUS	= 160-169
SUPERIOR RAYS IQ MAKES YOU ONE OF THE ALL-TIME GREATS	= 150-159
OUTSTANDING RAYS IQ THAT PLACES YOU AMONG THE TOP PLAYERS	= 140-149
ABOVE AVERAGE RAYS IQ THAT EARNS YOU A NICE PAYCHECK	= 130-139
SOLID RAYS IQ THAT LETS YOU PLAY BALL FOR A LIVING	= 120-129
AVERAGE RAYS IQ GOOD ENOUGH TO GET YOU TO THE SHOW	= 110-119
AVERAGE RAYS IQ GOT YOU A CUP OF COFFEE BUT THAT'S ALL	= 100-109

How'd you do? We'd like to know. Send us an email: tckrelliot@gmail.com

Tell us how many questions you got right, and if you scored high enough, you might just make your way onto a Hall of Fame list to be included in Volume II of Rays IQ.

If you enjoyed reading this book, please consider posting a review online at Amazon.com or wherever you buy books—and don't be shy about posting your Rays IQ!

Andy Sonnanstine

About the Authors

ANDREW MICHAEL (ANDY) SONNANSTINE is currently in his fifth year in Major League Baseball, all with the Tampa Bay Rays. A 13th-round draft pick in 2004, he has become a valued member of the Rays pitching staff that has won two of the last three American League East titles.

A native of Wadsworth, Ohio, Andy attended Kent State University and excelled on the diamond, setting single-season school records in wins, innings pitched and strikeouts as he led the Golden Flashes to the MAC Tournament title along with MVP honors in 2004.

Andy had a brief but standout minor league career, leading all Rays' farmhands in wins and strikeouts in 2005, and was named the organization's Pitcher of the Year after posting a 15-8 record with a 2.67 ERA in 2006. He made his major league debut on June 5, 2007 and gained his first major league win in his next start, beating the Florida Marlins by the score of 9-4 while striking out ten (including seven in a row) and going 2 for 3 at the plate. For the season, he ranked 5th among AL rookies with 22 starts and 130.2 innings pitched.

He had a breakout season in 2008, when he was a full-time starter on the Rays team that advanced to the World Series. During the regular season, he went 13-9 with a 4.38 ERA, and he made three starts in the playoffs, winning his first two, including the clinching Game 4 of the AL Division Series against the White Sox.

In 2009 Andy pitched out of the bullpen for the first time in his Major League career, a role he continued in 2010 as he led all Rays relievers in innings pitched as the Rays won the American League East title.

Not blessed with an overpowering fastball, Andy relies on athleticism, hard work and preparation to get hitters out. He has multiple pitches and he throws them with pinpoint control. Despite playing in the

American League, Andy also takes great pride in his hitting. He owns a career batting average of .348 (8-for-23), including the postseason. On May 17, 2009, due to a lineup mix-up, he was forced to bat third against the Cleveland Indians. He was the first pitcher to be in the starting lineup of an AL home game since 1976 ... and he went 1-for-3, with an RBI double.

He currently resides in St. Petersburg, Florida with his golden retriever Murphy.

TUCKER ELLIOT is a former high school athletic director and baseball coach who now writes fulltime. A native of Georgia, he now resides in Tampa and is a diehard fan of both the Braves and Rays.

Acknowledgements

ALONG WITH BLACK MESA PUBLISHING, I'd like to thank Dan Horwits and the Beverly Hills Sports Council for making this project a reality. I'd also like to thank Ellen McGlynn, who got this ball rolling for us and worked tirelessly no matter how many questions we sent her way.

As a writer, I've been fortunate to cross paths with many extraordinary people—and during the time Andy and I were collaborating on this book I was lucky enough to tag along with author Zac Robinson and legendary cutman Jacob "Stitch" Duran as they visited the Wounded Warrior Center at Landstuhl Regional Medical Center in Germany. I've loved baseball my whole life, but as Zac and Stitch were signing autographs and giving away books to our wounded service members it was a stark reminder of what it really means to be heroic. This is not an exhaustive list by any means, but I'm especially grateful to the following people who in some capacity serve and make our country great, and who also supported me with their friendship and encouragement as I worked on this and other projects:

Joe Soriano—who is also a stats guru and soon-to-be author;

Stacie Graves, Kim Coard, Felicia Raymundo, and Tom Yost—who do amazing work with little thanks for our military kids living overseas;

Aaliyah, Bea G-R, and Taylor—Babo told me to keep up my search for extraordinary, and then you guys came along; and incidentally, despite being a pseudo-Red Sox fan, Bea took the coolest picture ever of a Rays hat, and ... Taylor thinks the TB on the hat stands for *Taylor is a Beast*;

Sherrie—officially the "second" nicest person in the world, she's also the biggest Rays fan in Asia;

And finally, Lieutenant Colonel Bryan Huntsman, United States Air Force, his wife Carolyn and their children, Daniel, who may well be the next Albert Pujols, Lindsey, who is an aspiring author with considerable talent, and Steph, who wears her Rays hat with pride despite living in Mariners country ...

Tucker Elliot
Tampa, FL
March 2011

References

WEBSITES

Baseball-reference.com
MLB.com (and the official team sites through MLB.com)
BaseballHallofFame.org
ESPN.com

BOOKS

Baseball, an Illustrated History, Geoffrey C. Ward and Ken
      Burns
*The Team by Team Encyclopedia of Major League
      Baseball*, Dennis Purdy
The Unofficial Guide to Baseball's Most Unusual Records,
      Bob Mackin
The 2005 ESPN Baseball Encyclopedia, edited by Pete
      Palmer and Gary Gillette

About Black Mesa

Look for these other titles in the IQ Series:

- *Mixed Martial Arts (Volumes I & II)*
- *New York Yankees*
- *Atlanta Braves*
- *Boston Red Sox (Volumes I & II)*
- *Milwaukee Brewers*
- *St. Louis Cardinals*
- *Kansas City Royals*
- *Cincinnati Reds*
- *Major League Baseball*
- *Boston Celtics*
- *New England Patriots*
- *University of Texas Longhorns Football*
- *University of Oklahoma Sooners Football*
- *University of Florida Gators Football*
- *University of Georgia Bulldogs Football*

For information about special discounts for bulk purchases, please email:

black.mesa.publishing@gmail.com

www.blackmesabooks.com

28318452R10073

Made in the USA
Lexington, KY
13 December 2013